Barcelona

Editado por
A. CAMPAÑA
Pelayo, 60 - Barcelona 08001

VIKING, S.A. - Sta. Carolina, 79 - Barcelona 25

ISBN 84-300-0383-5
D. L. B. 43.363-1978

Photographs

Antonio Campañá
Juan Puig-Ferrán

designs   **Juan Soto**

BARC...

Mont Serat.

Mer   Medite...

A   *Le Mont Juif le guèt.*   E   *La Porte de la Ramble.*
B   *Bastion double de la Tersanne.*   F   *S.t François les Cordeliers.*
C   *S.te Marie Madrone.*   G   *Palais de Cardonne du Vice-Roy.*
D   *La Tersanne Arcenal.*   H   *La Merced.*

R   *S.te Catherine*   X   *Nostre-Dam...*
S   *La Douanne*   *ou le refuge.*
T   *La Place d'Armes*   Y   *Le Fanal du...*
V   *La Porte du Molle*   Z   4 *Tour de ...*

le Molle

Noſtre Dame del Pic.
Les grands Carmes.
La Sceau Eſueſché ou eſt le
Corps Sᵗᵉ Eularie Patronne.

N L'Inquiſition.
O La gallerie pres le Barreau.
P Le Barreau ou la ſalle des Caualiers.
Q Sᵗᵉ Marie de la Mer.

Mont Serrat
le.
ſs.

La Scituation de Barcelonne eſt
au regard du Cid de 4 0. d. 35. m. de lat.
et ſa longitude 22. d. 36. minutes.

The traditional Sardana dance groups competing in the Main Square of the Pueblo Español

A pair of intimate friends and great photographers — Campañá and Puig Ferrán — have together composed a magnificent book which constitutes the best possible eulogy one could make for Barcelona. They show us the city just as it is in a series of fine and at times really impressive photographs which reflect all the variety of this city that has justifiably been so fervently praised both by its own inhabitants and by foreigners.

With these photographs by Campañá and Puig Ferran we get the sensation that we are moving through the immense city from one end to the other. The Ramblas! The heart of Barcelona. The greatest attraction of the old part of the city. Its greatest charm. Historical synthesis and legitimate pride of the city. But it is not merely this part, marvellous though it is, which is such a symphony of colour for visitors; it is the unique attractiveness of the city as a whole. It is hard to say whether the city has

General view of the Port

changed into a garden, or whether Nature itself has become a city, for there are many lovely new zones in Barcelona — Pedralbes, Sarriá, Montjuic, Horta — pleasantly situated along the green foothills of the mountains, following the undulations of the terrain. To appreciate these incomparable suburbs to the full, one has to slip away from Campañá and Puig Ferrán and wander along solitary streets where the trees meet above us to form a cool, green, rustling canopy; one will have to wander through these high regions of the city close to the bright mountain summits above the blue see, where the city thins out and fades away into open country.

In the pages of this book, the authors have tried to capture the spirit of this great city; they express the essence of these streets, squares and history-filled corners in this fine photographic record. Each photograph shows a convergence of *ancient and modern. In these pages we see Barcelona in its entirety, a Barcelona where one finds, on the one hand, great business concerns, and on the other bull-fights and football watches; a Barcelona where great ocean liners dock, where the Big Wheel revolves on the Tibidabo, where hundreds of summer bathers relax on the beaches – all of this making Barcelona, as a great contemporary writer has said, the greatest and most European of Spanish cities.*

Years, or even centuries from now, someone will pick up this book in a forgotten library and it will surely count as a record of human values. Barcelona has continually adapted itself to technological advances whilst retaining at the same time a special poetic quality which has built itself up through the centuries.

José Tarin-Iglesias

Barcelona's very own
Canaletes drinking fountain

Like every great city, Barcelona contains numerous starting-
points or convergence-points amid its principal communications.
From among these various nerve-centres we are going to con-
cern ourselves first with the Plaza de Cataluña, nucleus of an
area of over 60 square kilometres with the two million plus
population which the Barcelona metropolis contains. It is a
cardinal point also for this guide, since it is from there that
we propose to take the tourist by the hand and, always using
Plaza Cataluña as our starting-point, show him everything of
interest in the city. It is possible to reconstruct twenty centuries
of history just from Barcelona's architecture and monuments;
both in ancient and modern art it can offer, among other things,
its collections of Romanesque art, unique in the world; the
Barrio Gótico (Gothic Quarter), exceptional for its proportions;
the Picasso Museum, unique to Barcelona, and the greatest and
most expressive achievements of the disconcerting genius of
Gaudí, in the vanguard of artistic achievement in both cases.
Of a different order there is its Parque Zoológico (Zoological
Gardens), daily more highly considered in the world; the zone
of international fairs and congresses, and the permanent but
progressive display of work and culture.

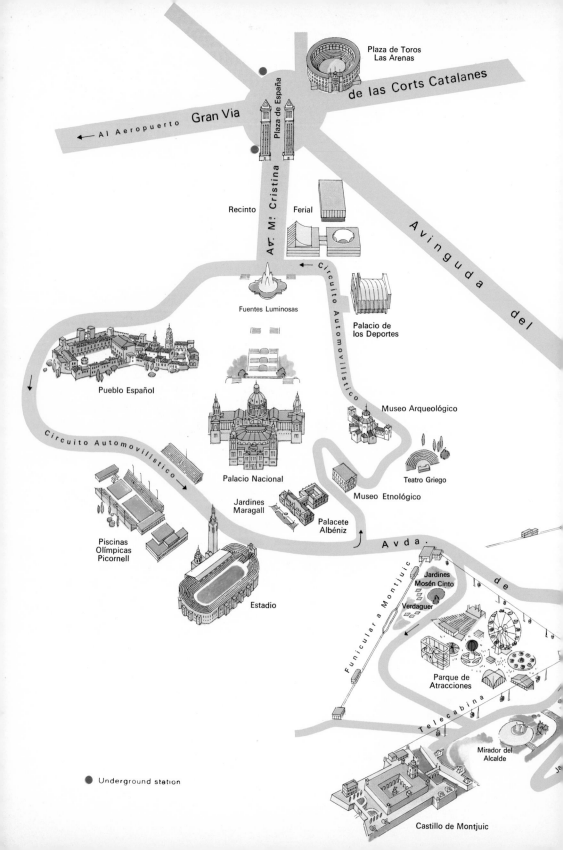

Plaza de Toros
Las Arenas

de las Corts Catalanes

← Al Aeropuerto   Gran Via

Plaza de España

Av. Mª Cristina

Avinguda del

Recinto   Ferial

Circuito Automovilístico

Fuentes Luminosas

Palacio de los Deportes

Pueblo Español

Museo Arqueológico

Circuito Automovilístico

Palacio Nacional

Museo Etnológico

Teatro Griego

Jardines Maragall

Palacete Albéniz

Avda.

Piscinas Olímpicas Picornell

Estadio

Funicular a Montjuic

de

Jardines Mosén Cinto Verdaguer

Parque de Atracciones

Telecabina

Mirador del Alcalde

● Underground station

Castillo de Montjuic

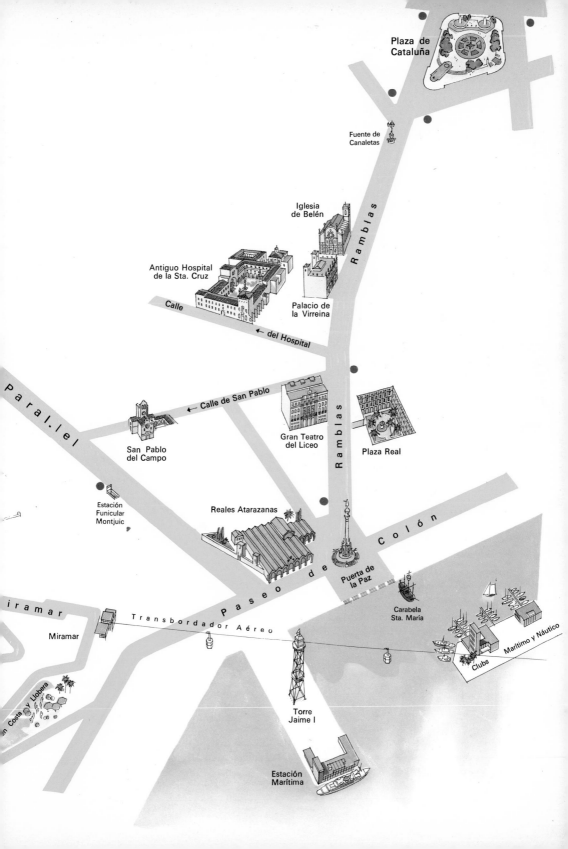

Plaza de
Cataluña

Fuente de
Canaletas

Ramblas

Iglesia
de Belén

Antiguo Hospital
de la Sta. Cruz

Palacio de
la Virreina

Calle

← del Hospital

Calle de San Pablo →

Ramblas

Gran Teatro
del Liceo

Plaza Real

San Pablo
del Campo

Parallel

Estación
Funicular
Montjuic

Reales Atarazanas

Paseo de Colón

Puerta de
la Paz

Carabela
Sta. María

Clubs

Marítimo y Náutico

iramar

Miramar

Transbordador Aéreo

Costa y Llobera

Torre
Jaime I

Estación
Marítima

Part of the Plaza de Cataluña
and the Paseo de Gracia

Parade of «majorettes»
along the Ramblas

A glance at the map of Barcelona is sufficient to make one realise immediately that the Plaza de Cataluña represents a point of union between the old and new parts of the city. Nine of the most important transport routes lead into it : the Ramblas, Rambla de Cataluña, Paseo de Gracia, Ronda de la Universidad and of San Pedro; Avenida Puerta del Angel and Pelayo, Vergara and Fontanella streets. Banking establishments are plentiful in these streets, almost encircling the Plaza de Cataluña completely, which thus becomes for Barcelona what the City is for London. The remaining buildings round the square are occupied by big retail stores, restaurants, bars, cafés and other public establishments. Two important underground railway stations, two of the

metro system, and numerous bus-stops on the surface all mean
that this square is one of the most crowded spots in the city.
Trees, flower-beds, fountains and sculptures are in the centre
of the square whose decoration is the work of the architect
Nebot. Facing the Ramblas in one of these flower-beds is one
of the loveliest pieces of sculpture in the city : «The Goddess»
by Josep Clará. The other statues are by the artists Otero,
Borrell, Nicolau, Luciano Oslé, Miguel Oslé, Arnau, Llimona,
Gargallo, Casanovas, Navarro, Dunyach and Viladomat. Leaving
the Plaza de Cataluña behind us, we are going to start on our
first itinerary, heading towards the Port by the Rambla or Ramblas.
Going down this vitally important artery of the city, not only

The Rambla
and Canaletes fountain

do we discover the most picturesque and typical aspect of Barcelona's physiognomy, but we also enjoy a spectacle which is unforgettable in its originality and charm. This is why Barcelona's Ramblas have become world-famous. The novelist Somerset Maugham, non-stop traveller that he was, said of them : «It is the most beautiful street in the world». Really it consists of a harmonious, spontaneous, almost magical combination of changing colour and light, whether by day or night. This effect is produced by the hundreds of plain trees lining the central promenade and forming a cupola of infinitely varying greens, the home of thousands of chirruping sparrows; by the stalls selling birds of all classes; by the marvellous Rambla de las Flores, a feast of colour and scents and a worthy rival of Paris's «Marché de Fleurs» and Rome's Piazza d'Espagna; by the newspaper kiosks, real open-air libraries; by the fascination of the passers-by; and − an essential element − the continual coming and going of people of all classes and countries, people who may be hurrying about their daily tasks, or merely idling the time away, but all of them apparently happy and cheerful just from being on Barcelona's Rambla. This popular grand parade came into being when a wide avenue was constructed over the old water-course, or «rámla» to·use the Arabic term, which led down here towards the sea. It is supposed that the present word «Rambla» comes from this expression. On the

The bird-seller's
stalls in the Rambla

left of this water-course rose the fortified walls of the medieval
town, and on the right was open country where a large number
of extra-mural convents came to be built. It is along these two
edges of the «rámla» or «rambla» that the houses which today
form the Ramblas were subsequently built : buildings today
filled with banks, offices, hotels, cafés, bars, restaurants and
other establishments where you can buy everything. Their decoration, the brightly-lit shop-windows at night play their part
in the dazzling, special appeal of the Ramblas. As soon as you
start walking down them you are almost bound to stop in front
of the Canaletas Fountain. Spaniards and foreigners have spread
the fame of its water so that the drinking-fountain has become
on of the symbols of Barcelona. Shall we stop and try the water
which comes from its taps, so running the risk of falling under
the legendary spell according to which «Whoever drinks water
from the Fuente de Canaletas will remain and live for ever in
Barcelona»?

Part of the
Rambla de las Flores

The first building which can claim our attention is the Aca-
demy of Sciences. It is not unusual to see Barcelona residents
putting their watches right by the clock on its façade under the
impression that this, of all clocks, should certainly always be
right. Further down, we find the church of Belén, a fine example
of Baroque style. It was constructed between 1681 and 1729
to the designs of Barcelona's Josep Juli. On the other side is
the Palacio Moya, better known as the Palacio Comillas, built
in 1771 by Cayetano Luis de Copons, with paintings by El

General view of the mass
of colour on the Rambla
de las Flores

Vigatá and Flaugier in the salons. During the Napoleonic occu-
pation, General Duchesne lived in this palace, and it was he
who had the present trees on the Ramblas brought from the
Dehesa of Gerona whose trees had in their turn been planted
by the French. In the Rambla de las Flores we find what is
perhaps the most important building architecturally of the whole
promenade : the Virreina. Construction of this was begun in
1772 and finished in 1784, the work being directed by the
sculptor Carles Grau. The promoter was Felipe Manuel Amat
y de Junyent who was viceroy in Peru for over fifteen years.
When he came back to Barcelona in 1779 at the age of 74
years, he married María Francisca Fivaller, who was soon left

Different aspects of the
marvellously colourful
Rambla de las Flores

Façade of the Palacio de la Virreina, today the Museum of Decorative Arts

a widow. It was this Fivaller who, in spite of never having fulfilled any viceregal role, gave the name «La Virreina» to the building. It was subsequently acquired by the Council and today serves as a home for the Museum of Decorative Arts and monographic exhibitions. At the end of the Rambla de las Flores we find ourselves in front of the Gran Teatro del Liceo, with a rather discreet entrance in comparison with the significance and interior of the building : it is one of the biggest and finest opera houses in the world, as famous for its perfomances as La Scala in Milan

What was formerly the
«Pla de la Boqueria»
on the Rambla

and Covent Garden in London. The construction, following the project of Miguel Garriga y Roca, was finished in 1848. Because of a fire, it had to be rebuilt in 1862, under the direction of Oriol Mestres, and was decorated with paintings by Martí Alsina, Mestres, Casas and Tigalt. It is notable for the good taste throughout and excellent conditions, as an example of which we can mention the acoustics in the theatre itself, which have been classified as perfect. There are 3,500 seats on the main floor which is surrounded by stalls, boxes and superimposed circles, the whole forming a marvellous work of art. This trip would be incomplete without a little detour to the old «Hospital de la Santa Cruz», an interesting collection of successive architectural styles. It owes its origin to the fusion of four hospitals — two of them religious and two run by the city — into one, in 1401, utilising the hospital which had been established on this spot by Canon Colom in 1229. In 1638 the group of buildings was badly damaged by fire but once the repairs had been made most of the original buildings were conserved, corresponding to those which are there today. All the hospital services have been transferred to more modern buildings in other parts of the city and the old Hospital de la Santa Cruz now serves as a home for the Cataluña or Central Library, with nearly a million volumes, including three hundred printed before the sixteenth century, and over two thousand manuscripts of great historical and literary value; the Escuela Massana Fine Arts School, Conservatorio Municipal de Artes Suntuarias; the Escuela de Bibliotecarias (Librarians' School); exhibition rooms and other cultural and artistic institutions. The central patio is an unexpected haven of peace and silence. Three great halls frame this patio which is surrounded almost completely, by porticos and presided over by a cross mounted on a twisted column. Adjoining the central nucleus are the old buildings of the Casa de Convalecencia and of the College of Surgery, today the Academia de Medicina. In the entrance-hall, patio, staircase and chapel of the Casa de Convalecencia there are a number of attractive ceramic tiles, work of Llorenç Passoles who was as good a ceramic artist as he was bad as a draughtsman. The architecture of the patio is neoclassical, with the exception of the fountain in the middle, which is baroque and is surmounted by a statue of St.Paul by the Frenchman Lluis Bonifaci (died 1697) who was resident in Barcelona. In the chapel there are paintings by Antoni Viladomat, the best artist of the 18th century Catalan school. The College of Surgery was built in 1762 and is a fine example of the neoclassical style, with the simple, well-balanced line of its façade. Outstanding in the interior is the amphitheatre or lecture hall, elliptical in form and richly decorated. The original marble

The artistry and luxury of the stalls, boxes and upper circles of the Gran Teatro del Liceo

Patio of the old
Hospital de la Santa
Cruz, today the
home of cultural
institutions

A performance in the
Gran Teatro del Liceo

table for anatomy lessons can still be seen. Neither can we
forget to visit the church of San Pablo del Campo at the end
of the street of the same name. It is a Romanesque church
dating from the beginning of the 12th century, laid out in the
form of a Greek cross, barrel-vaulted and with the dome of this
period. The main doorway has some Merovingian capitals of the
7th and 8th centuries; Inside is Guifred II's stone (died 911).
This shows that there was a Benedictine community on this

The Romanesque church
of San Pablo del Campo.
Cloisters and exterior view

The typical and
romantic Plaza Real

spot, leading one to suppose that the old building was destroyed at the time of Almanzor and that subsequent rebuilding took advantage of the remains of the original convent. The 13th century cloisters and the 14th century rectorial house (originally the Chapter House) are admirable. Back again in the Ramblas, it is necessary to go into the Plaza Real (Royal Square), which takes its inspiration from French cities of the Napoleonic period, neoclassical in style. It is the work of the notable architect Daniel Molina, who was responsible for various constructions in the city, such as the houses — also with porticos — surrounding the Mercado de la Boquería in the Rambla de las Flores. The slender palm trees, the flower-beds, the central fountain, flanked by lamp-standards designed by that genius Gaudí, the balanced quadrilateral formed by the whole square, make the Plaza Real a wonderfully peaceful spot. Sunday mornings it is the centre for a busy little stamp-collectors' market. Immediately opposite the Plaza Real, Conde del Asalto street leads out into the Ramblas. A few paces down here we find the Palacio del Conde Güell, one of the most fantastic creations of Gaudí. At present this original example of Gaudí's architecture contains the Historical Museum of the Theatre. And talking of theatre, continuing down the Ramblas, we come to the Plaza del Teatro, former centre of the scenic art when it was at its zenith in Barcelona around the turn of the century. Of those far-off triumphs of actors and authors, all that is left today is the old Teatro Principal, in bad repair, and the monument to Federico Soler alias Serafí Pitarra, promoter of the Catalan theatre. The monument is the work of Pedro Falqués and the statue of Agustín Querol. Serafí Pitarra, who seems to be waiting for the arrival of the crowds who applauded him so much, has his back to calle de Escudellers, a street with a special reputation because of the assorted crowd of people who go there, searching for amorous adventures or a lively evening, and because of its typical restaurants, bars and taverns. But Calle Escudellers really comes into its own in the evening and at night, just like certain districts and streets in Paris or Marseilles for example. Further down, after the Plaza del Teatro, is the Palacio Marc, built in 1776 as the residence of a distinguished, old family from Reus. Later on, the Bank of Spain moved in, and today another official body uses it. At the end of the Ramblas, as well as finding several extremely interesting buildings we are able to realise what have been and still are the principal factors which have made the Barcelona metropolis famous. In front of us is the extensive, clear and luminous panorama of the harbour, with its loading and unloading installations, the many ships of all classes, and the sea opening its wide horizon before our gaze. Among the installations mentioned we should mention the modern Estación Marítima, the old Swimming Club, with its indoor pool, at the beginning of the

Puerta de la Paz.
Columbus's monument,
with the ship «Santa
María» in the foreground

General view of the Port and Paseo de Colón (Columbus Parade)
with the mountain of Montjuic in the background

The harbour. Aerial view of the Bosch, Alsina and España wharves

Another view of the harbour, this time the Barcelona wharf

Paseo de la Escollera. At the same spot there is the striking «escultura, símbolo marinero» (sculpture, marine symbol) the work of Subirachs. Opposite this monument is the building housing the Instituto de Investigaciones Pesqueras, where there is a notable aquarium specialising in fauna of the Mediterranean. In the same Paseo (Parade) almost at the end, a «monumental remate de hierro» a work of abstract art in iron by the sculptor Aulestia, has been installed. Dotted around the harbour we find the Royal Maritime Club, the Nautical Club, the Astilleros (shipyards), the Fishermen's Wharf — an invaluable model for innumerable painters —, and the Zona Franca, used preferentially by shipping from all latitudes. The Ramblas open out widely onto the Puerta de la Paz square. Other important throughfares which lead into this square are Avenida Morato, Avinguda del Paral·lel, the road to Can Tunis and the access road to the mountain of Montjuic; the Paseo de Colón and Anselmo Clavé street. Later we shall described in detail the buildings which surround

The Santa Madrona
entrance gateway in the
XVth century wall

Panorama over the harbour and the
Maresme coastline from Montjuic mountain

this nerve-centre. In the centre is the monument to Columbus, reproductions of which have almost become a symbol of Barcelona. It was inaugurated in June 1888, after being constructed to the plans of Cayetano Buigas and decorated with sculpture by Nobas, Pagés and Serratosa, Atché and Fuxá. It is 59 metres high and the statue of the sailor measures 7.60 metres. A lift goes up the interior of the column to the top from which we get a wide panorama of the city and harbour. Tied up to the wharf at the foot of the monument is the reproduction of the «Santa María», flagship of Columbus's first expedition to America. This disembarkation point was opened in 1849 when it received the name Puerta de la Paz (Door of Peace) which it still bears in commemoration of the peace achieved by General Concha in the «guerra del matiners». From that date on, the construction of the «Puerto Marítimo» went forward with real impetus. From the simple anchorage of the Phonecians and the Greeks, through the natural basin of medieval

A corner of the «Costa y Llobera» garden in Montjuic Park

Panorama over the city
from the top station of
the aerial cable-car
on Montjuic

times and the primitive rock-wharves of the 15th century, improved in 1477, we come to the true bases of the present-day harbour of Barcelona, thanks to the reforms directed by the Greek Estagis first, and subsequently by Barcelona's own José Rafo. Thus the way was opened to reach the present-day total area of fifty hectares with three hundred and forty hectares of sheltered water. The port has the merit of being completely artificial, showing what an effort the Barcelona people made to develop something which is so important for expansion of commerce and tourism. One of the best additions to the harbour is the Paseo Marítimo, the Marine Parade. This is an achievement of

Monument to the
«Sardana» by José
Cañas in the gardens
on Montjuic

the present City Council and it brings the city into closer contact
with the sea. It begins in the Barceloneta, the maritime quarter
par excellence of Barcelona. This popular and crowded district
on the eastern side of the port was contructed to provide homes
for those rendered homeless by the disappearance of the old
Ribera district. Construction began in February 1753, following
the plans of Próspero de Verboon, with the streets in straight
lines and the houses limited to single-storey buildings. But in
1837 the Baron de Meer authorised the addition of another
storey to each building. The parish church of the Barceloneta
is the work of Pedro Carmeño; inside it is the sepulchre containing the remains of the capitán general marqués de Mina who
ordered the construction of this quarter which certainly represents the first example of town-planning in Barcelona. Most of
its original, special appearance has been conserved until today.
Each street, whether horizontal or vertical, has its authentically
picturesque aspect. Even the people, apparently different from
Barcelona's other inhabitants, seem to retain the best virtues
of sea-people; inveterate optimism, vigorous nobility and good
humour tempered with sceptical irony. On the beach there are
all the usual bathing establishments and crowds of people,
especially during the hot months of the year. Picturesque bars,

taverns and restaurants serving typical coastal village foods are scattered through the streets and the Paseo Nacional. The district has acquired so much prestige that, whereas only a little while ago it was known merely to a few lovers of typical sea-foods, today it is a centre of attraction for an enormous number of tourists. Of the buildings around Plaza de la Paz, on the left there is one which was used for casting cannons in the XVIIth century, was the Banco de Barcelona from 1844, then Comandancia de Somatenes (Armed Police) de Cataluña, and is now used by the Army; and there is also the modern building of the Gobierno Militar and Junta de Obras del Puerto y Policía del Puerto; on the right, in another modern building, is the Comandancia de Marina, the Customs building, work of Enric Sagnier, finished in 1902, and — historically and architecturally outstanding — the group of buildings comprising the old Dressanes or Atarazanas (shipyards). This is a construction unique of its kind in the world for there is no other non-religious building which is so well-preserved and majestically complete. It was Peter II (1239-1285) who, because of the ever-growing amount of maritime transport through Barcelona, ordered the amplification of the installations which his predecessor James I (1208-1276) had had built on this spot for the construction and repair of ships. But it was Peter III (1319-1387) who had the shipyards brought up to their present grandiose proportions, capable of accommodating 30 galleys in simultaneous construction. Most of the ships used for trading with the Orient and for the Catalan dominion of the Mediterranean from the XIVth to the XVIIth century came from these yards. They were the property of the Council of One Hundred until 1390 when they were handed over to the «Generalitat», which, in turn, handed

The Castle of Montjuic, today the «Museo Histórico Militar»

Fountain in the gardens of the «Mirador del Alcalde» (Mayor's Look-out Point) in Montjuic Park

Entrance to the old
Castle of Montjuic,
home of the Museo
Histórico Militar

them over to the Army in 1663. From 1792 until 1936 they
were used as an Artillery barracks and for instruction. They were
then returned to the City and became a Maritime Museum
which has become of the greatest importance because of the
quantity and quality of the material it contains. Behind the
Atarazanas one can see, at the beginning of the Avinguda del
Paral·lel, part of the old 15th century walls, with the only
remaining gateway, that of Santa Madrona. Set among the
already-described harbour installations are two high towers used
by an aerial cable-car linking the part of the harbour where the
breakwater begins with the gardens of Montjuic. Here, another
telecabin system has been installed to carry passengers to the
top of this mountain by a continuous cabin service. Whether
by these means or by the road which leads off Puerta de la Paz,
we recommend the tourist to pay a visit to the mountain of
Montjuic, which we have mentioned repeatedly; for here on
Montjuic most of the reasons for visiting Barcelona await him.
And this is quite apart from the history of the mountain itself,

with its castle, in spite of its varying correlation with that of the city. Montjuic today is far removed from the Iberian city of Laya which was situated there; lost in the mists of time also is the temple which the Romans built there to their god Jupiter. Some historians say the name of the mountain comes from Jupiter : Mons Jovis, Monte de Júpiter, Montjuic. There are other authorities who say that nearer our own time there was a Jewish cemetery on the mountain which was therefore called Mons Judaico; and others again that the name was given because of the great fame and influence in the city life of the members of a Hebrew family called Mont Judaic. However, with presentday Montjuic we must begin by stressing the historical and archaeological value of the castle, given by the Army to the City, and, once restored to its original state, converted into a Military History Museum. All of this is largely thanks to the enthusiasm and effort of Barcelona's present Mayor. Notwithstanding this speciality, the Museum contains an unusual variety of very valuable collections of all kinds. This is sufficient to prove that since the look-out point of the primitive Iberians

Another view of the entrance to the old castle of Montjuic

The «Mosen Cinto Verdaguer» and
«Joan Maragall» garden in Montjuic Park

Garden and Palacete
Albéniz in Montjuic Park

there has always existed a more or less important fortress on the summit. The present one is basically 17th century, enlarged considerably in the 18th and with reforms during subsequent epochs. Because of the great affection the people of Barcelona have always felt for the mountain of Montjuic, they can be proud of the fact that today it is better than it has ever been. Well-laid out parks and gardens alternate with the natural vegetation of the mountain and the steep slopes give exciting possibilities to landscape gardeners. The city's «Servicio Municipal de Parques y Jardines» continues to do good work here, ably assisted in its task of beautifying Montjuic by José María Porcioles, mayor of the city since 1958. Worthy of the tourist's attention are the improved gardens of Miramar, Laribal, La

Rosalera and the Font del Gat; and the completely new Mirador del Alcalde, a veritable balcony on the Mediterranean, which is the work of Luis Riudor assisted by Joaquim M. Casamor, with paving by Josep Tharrats and fountains by Carlos Buigas. Near the latter is the Parque de Atracciones (Fun-fair), the biggest and most modern installation of this kind in the city. Nearby we find the monument to the Sardana (Catalonia's famous folk-dance), the work of the sculptor José Cañas. Another new garden is that dedicated to the poet Mosén Cinto Verdaguer. It contains a statue in memory of the poet by the artist J. Sabi. The special feature of this garden is its collection of bulbous plants which constitute a living exhibition. Another garden is named after the poet Costa y Llobera and contains a monument dedicated to him, symbolising his celebrated poem «Pi de Formentor», the last verse of which is engraved on the monument. This is the work of the sculptor Ros Bofarull. This garden is notable for its very complete exhibition of succulents (cactus, etc.). Another original garden is that called «Jardín Joan Maragall» which has a marvellous display of evergreens. It was created along classical lines but with the special feature of sculptures by Teófilo Berrau, Joan Rebull, Josep Viladomat,

View of the Palacio
Nacional from the
Greek pergola in the
Albéniz Gardens

Enrique Monjo, Federico Marés, María L. Granero, Eulalia Fá-
bregas de Sentmenat, Ernest Maragall and J. Tey. The architect
Dr Joaquim M. Casamor designed and supervised the preparation
of all these gardens, with the collaboration of the technical
architect Antonio Solán and the technical engineer Miguel
Crespo. As well as the undoubted technical mastery displayed,
the artistic taste is exceptional. The Joan Maragall garden was
designed for gatherings of a festive or social character and
contains a special theatre for this purpose. The process of
beautifying the mountain was begun in 1929 with the «Exhibition
Gardens», designed by the Frenchman Forestier, which contain
an extensive and modern zone for industrial fairs. Here there
are annual congresses and exhibitions continually, of all kinds,
with such frequency that Barcelona has been called «City of
Industrial Fairs and Congresses». There are four storeys over a

Aerial view of part of
the Pueblo Español
(Spanish village)

floor area of about 15,000 square metres, with various «palaces»
and other suitable buildings, as well as magnificent rest and
recreation areas. One of these buildings is the Palace of Nations
which has a hall capable of accommodating congresses of up
to 1,500. This zone owes much of its importance also to the
modernity of all its services, offering almost unlimited possibilities.
Another example of the enhancement of Montjuic's beauty is
offered by the Palacete (Little Palace) Albéniz. Intended as an
honorary residence for distinguished visitors, it has been taste-
fully reformed and enlarged; the elegant nobility and discreet
luxury of the changes add new qualities to those it already
possessed. These qualities can be found both in the exterior
and interior of the Palace as well as in the gardens surrounding
it. The architects responsible were Ros de Ramis. Ignacio Serra-
goday and Antonio Lozoya. Among the works of art inside the
Palacete Albéniz are paintings by Nonell, Casas, Rusiñol, Martí
Alsina, Baixeras, Vayreda, Muños de Pablos and Dalí. In other
parts of the mountain may be found the Teatro Griego, for open-

air performances of classical works with accommodation for nearly 2,000 spectators, the Museo Arqueológico and Museo Etnológico; the Gran Estadio (Stadium) Municipal, the new Estadio de la Fuxarda, the Palacio de los Deportes which, as well as being used for sporting events, is also used for festivals and competitions of singing and music; a large winter-garden, the Municipal Swimming Pool in the Laribal Gardens and the Picornell Swimming Pool, recently inaugurated for the internationally famous European Swimming Championships which represented a great success for the city of Barcelona. We could extend this list, mentioning other installations and buildings. Of these the Pueblo Español (Spanish Village) deserves a chapter all to itself. It is a great urban nucleus in which architectural solutions from North and South, from mountain and coast, from all parts of the Iberian peninsular, have been brought together. We owe a great debt to the artists Xavier Nogués, Miguel Utrillo and Ramón Raventós who conceived the idea of this «pueblo» and put it into effect in 1927. It is now world famous for its uniqueness, in spite of imitations which have been constructed in other cities. One enters the village through the San Vicents gate in

Puerta de Avila, main entrance to the Pueblo Español

The Main Square in the
Pueblo Español seen from
the Sangüesa porticoes

End of the Calle de
Cervantes in the
Pueblo Español

Pueblo Español. Plazuela
de la Iglesia (little square
of the church), Utebo

Prades Square and Fountain
in the Pueblo Español

Pueblo Español. Hermandad Square. Below: Santiago steps

the wall of Avila which surrounds the whole. Immediately in front of one is the Castellana Square; on the right are buildings in the style of Cáceres, opposite, through the Sangüesa arcade, the Plaza Mayor (Main Square). This latter is made up of buildings in the styles of Aragón, Burgos, Navarra, Catalonia, Soria, Castilia, etc., and is presided over by the Valderrobres Town Hall. At the back on the left, the steps of Santiago surround a group of Galician houses. Caballeros street, evoking Castilian villages, leads off from the other side of this square, and from

A Sardana Competition, the
thousand-year-old Catalan dance,
in the Main Square of the
Pueblo Español

The august presence
of the two Giants in the
same square

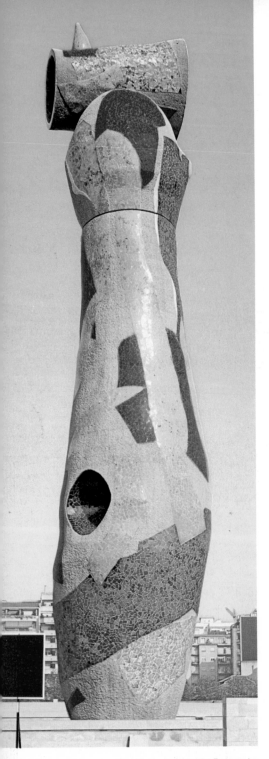

Monolito en la Plaza del Escorxador
de Joan Miró y azulejos
de Llorens-Artigas

El Palacio de Congresos

Fundación Miró

the Arco de Maya, Príncipe de Viana street recalls Navarran Basque architecture. In the Aragonesa Square is the bell-tower of Utebo, and then the Andalusian and Catalonian districts begin, with the streets of los Arcos, las Bulas, and la Davallada, Mercaders and Square of the Prades Fountain respectively. The gate in the wall which faces the sea is the Portal de Bové, Montblanc style. Valencia and Murcia are also represented around the street of Levante. Outside the walls there is a Romanesque Monastery and church in the style of the Catalonian Pyrenees. In the Plaza Mayor there is a Museo de Industrias

Pueblo Español.
Calle de Caballeros

y Artes Populares. This square often serves as a setting for festivals, folklore competitions and children's shows. In various parts of the «village» are establishments where arts and crafts are practised before the public gaze. Going up the promenade in front of the Pueblo Español and just a little further on, there

Plaza Castellana
at the entrance to the
Pueblo Español

Pueblo Español. Calle
del Alcalde de Zalamea

is a magnificent viewpoint looking out over the plain and delta
of the Llobregat as far as the cliffs of Garraf. At this look-out
point there is a statue of St.George on horse back. It is cast
in bronze and is another fine example of the work of Josep
Llimona. We still have to visit the Palacio Nacional, on the upper
floor of which is the Museo de Cerámica and the Throne Room,
decorated by Francisco Labarta and with paintings by Francisco
Galí. The centre of the Palace is occupied by an enormous hall
with accommodation for 4,000 seated persons, plus an upper
amphitheatre for several hundred more, also seated. It has one
of the biggest organs in Europe; it has 11,000 pipes, 154 combinations and 6 manual keyboards plus one foot-operated one.
But the real importance of the Palacio Nacional comes from
the fact that it contains the Museo de Arte de Cataluña the
main part of which consists of collections of Romanesque and
Gothic art. These collections are the most important in the world,

On this and the previous page, the part
where industrial fairs and congresses
are held, with the Magic Fountain
displaying various of its water and colour
combinations. In the background, the city
as far as its boundary marked by the Tibidabo

are indeed unique for the beautiful examples of 9th to 13th
century art. Frescos, murals, frontals and other liturgical objects
form what is perhaps the most valuable part of the Romanesque
series; the Gothic part contains a marvellous collection of retables
and carvings among which there are fine examples of the work
of such great masters as Huguet, Vergós, Dalmau, Serra, Borrassá,
Tintoretto, Ribera and Zurbarán. In front of the Palacio Nacional
and as a sort of finishing-touch to the Avenida María Cristina,
we can admire the famous illuminated fountains of Montjuic,
the Fuente Mágica. A masterpiece of engineering applied to
every possible combination of water and light, it is the work
of Carlos Buigas. The central basin is 1.8m. deep, is oval in

Pantocrator
Museo de Arte
de Cataluña

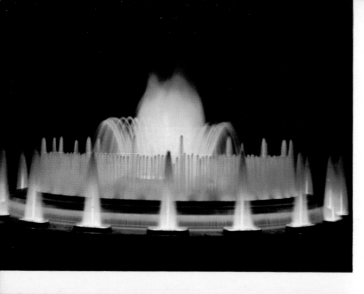

These pages show different moments in the ever-changing combinations of water and light of the illuminated fountains in the gardens of Montjuic, unique for their magical beauty, their variety of colour, and the grandeur of the spectacle they offer

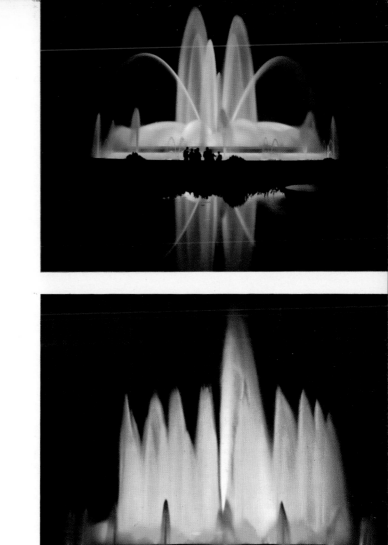
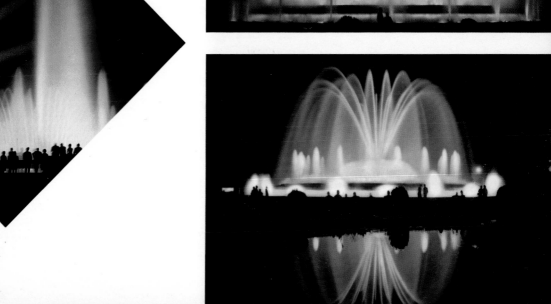

General view of Montjuic's industrial
fairs part, showing the fine surroundings

Plaza de España.
Entrance to the
Industrial Fairs and
Congresses part of
the Montjuic gardens

form, 65m. long and 50 wide. It contains two smaller basins, the lower one 35 m. in diameter, and the upper 12 m. The rate of flow is 2,430 litres per second and the central jet can reach a height of 50 metres. There are 28 different combinations of water and by combining these with each other and with the different lighting effects the resulting range of variations is almost infinite. The motors necessary for driving the pumps and ventilators are 1,413 h.p. The water is illuminated by 4,730 lamps with ten-colour filters and a power of 1,445 kilowatts. The fountain is directed by remote control from a cabin overlooking it. At night, when the marvellous colour-combinations of the fountain can best be appreciated, a fan of powerful searchlight beams, white or on occasion red, shine upwards from behind the Palacio Nacional. A different aspect of the mountain is the prestige which Montjuic has acquired for the car and motor-cycle races which are held on its circuit periodically. The Mont-juic Race Track is internationally famous and has been proclaimed as ideal for all kinds of motorised vehicles, whatever their power or characteristics. The same thing has happened with respect to bicycle racing : in the long history of this sport, the name of the Montjuic Track has become a tradition. Leaving the mountain by the Avenida María Cristina we come out into Plaza España, another important traffic centre of the city. On the left is the Air Terminal for Iberia and the other companies; opposite, on the other side of the square, is the bull-ring Plaza de Toros Las Arenas. It was built in 1900 and can accommodate 15,000 spectators, but we shall return to the spectacle of bull-fighting later. The three big red-brick buildings flanking this square were hotels at the time of the international Exhibition in 1929; today, one of them is a school and the other two are used for official purposes. The monument in the centre of Plaza de España is the work of the architect Jujol and is decorated with statues by Oslé. The most important of these latter are the ones placed on each of the three sides and representing the three seas which wash the coasts of the Iberian Peninsula : the Medi-terranean, the Atlantic and the Cantabrian.

Plaza de Cataluña. In the foreground
Josep Clará's «La Diosa» (Goddess)
in her marvellously floral setting

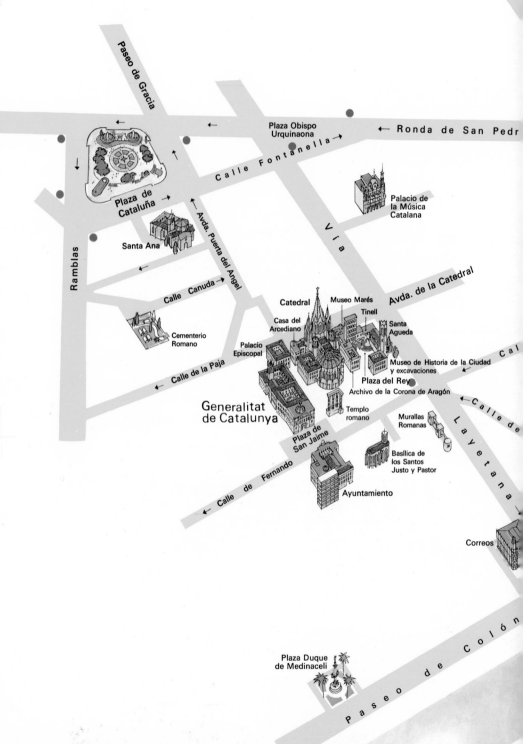

Paseo de Gracia

Plaza Obispo
Urquinaona

← Ronda de San Pedr

Calle Fontanella

Via

Palacio de
la Música
Catalana

Plaza de
Cataluña →

Santa Ana

Ramblas

Avda. Puerta del Angel

Calle Canuda →

Avda. de la Catedral

Catedral

Museo Marés

Tinell

Santa
Agueda

Casa del
Arcediano

Cementerio
Romano

Palacio
Episcopal

Museo de Historia de la Ciudad
y excavaciones

← Calle de la Paja

Plaza del Rey

Archivo de la Corona de Aragón

Generalitat
de Catalunya

Templo
romano

Murallas
Romanas

Plaza de
San Jaime

Basílica de
los Santos
Justo y Pastor

Calle de Fernando

Cal

Calle de Layetana

Ayuntamiento

← Calle de Fernando

Correos

Paseo de Colón

Plaza Duque
de Medinaceli

Paseo de Colón

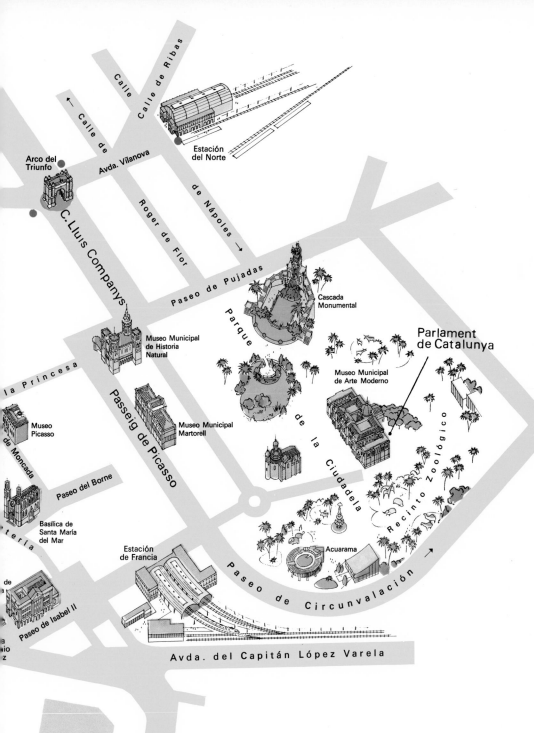

Calle de Ribas

Calle

Calle de

Estación
del Norte

Arco del
Triunfo

Avda. Vilanova

de Nápoles

C. Lluis Companys

Roger de Flor

Paseo de Pujadas

Cascada
Monumental

Parlament
de Catalunya

Museo Municipal
de Historia
Natural

Parque

Museo Municipal
de Arte Moderno

la Princesa

Passeig de Picasso

Museo Municipal
Martorell

de la Ciudadela

Recinto Zoológico

de Moncada

Museo
Picasso

Paseo del Borne

Basilica de
Santa María
del Mar

Estación
de Francia

Acuarama

z

Paseo de Isabel II

Paseo de Circunvalación

Avda. del Capitán López Varela

● Underground station

Church of the old
Colegiata de Santa Ana

In Plaza Cataluña again, we begin our trip to the oldest part of the city. We start off with a visit to what is left of the old Colegiata de Santa Ana, the church and the cloisters. It is situated behind the Banco de España and other buildings on the lower side of the Plaza Cataluña. The main entrance, the cloisters, and other traces of Gothic style make the visit worthwhile. Not far away, in the Villa de Madrid square, at the foot of the modernised façade of the Ateneo Barcelonés, one can see the remains of the 2nd Century Roman Cemetery. The tombs one sees here are an example of the Roman custom of burying their dead at the roadside in the centres of their cities. More towards the heart of the old Barcino is the church of the Basílica del Pino, whose exterior is the simplest and severest Catalan Gothic. A solidly-constructed octagonal belfry rises to a height of 54 metres. The church has two entrances around which one can still see traces of the early Romanesque church which existed on the same site. Over the main entrance, which gives onto the Plaza del Pino, there is a rose-window with marvellous tracery which is beaten for sheer size only by that of Nôtre Dame de Paris. The interior consists of just one nave divided into five ojives, each with side chapels between the pillars. The door opening onto the Plaza Beato Oriol is of the 13th century. From the Plaza del Pino we must go to the Barrio Gótico (Gothic Quarter) which we reach by the calle de la Paja. This street is a delight as it retains all its original qualities and is characterised by numerous antique and second-hand book shops. At the other end we come out into the Plaza Nueva, New Square, perhaps the oldest in Barcelona and the real entrance to the Barrio Gótico, the old quarter known as Mons Taber in medieval texts. It is right at the heart of the Pía Barcino of the first century Romans from which the name Barcelona possibly comes. The first things which attract one's attention in the Plaza Nueva are the two Roman towers which gave access to the walled part which was the only defence of the town from the 2nd to the 13th centuries. Contrasting with the antiquity of the rest of the square is the Colegio de Arquitectos building, with its functional style and its friezes decorated with graffiti by Picasso, the greatest innovator among contemporary artists. In these friezes Picasso has synthesised scenes from Catalonian folklore in rapid sketches. To the right of the Roman towers is the Palacio Episcopal, the Bishop's Palace, built over the wall in the 13th century. The façade which gives onto the Plaza Nueva however was added in the 18th century and is thus of Baroque style. Inside the patio of Romanesque construction is interesting. It has been carefully and intelligently restored. On the first floor, the «salón de honor», with paintings by El Vigatá is outstanding, and there are also some Romanesque traces. On the left-hand side of the towers, using the massive blocks of the wall as its foundations, is the Casa del Arcediano, today the Archivo Histórico de la Ciudad, with over 100,000 volumes and thousands of other documents. It was originally constructed in the 11th century to the orders of the Archdeacon Lluís Desplá, who had his residence there. Towards the end of the 15th century it was completely transformed, acquiring its present Renaissance-

Remains of the 2nd century Roman cemetery in the Plaza de Madrid

Plaza Nueva. Part of the façade of the Colegio
de Arquitectos, with a frieze by Picasso and
paintings by Miró. In the background the
Cathedral and rear façade of the
Archdeacon's house

Gothic structure. Noteworthy are the slender windows with their
sobre sculptured decorations, and the entrance, a model of
balanced composition. Admirable also is the porticoed patio
with its tall palm tree, the lovely fountain in the centre and the
discreet staircase leading to the upper floor. There are three
façades, one on the calle del Obispo, one on the Plaza de la
Catedral, and the third on the calle de Santa Lucía. Opposite
the last of these is the Capilla de Santa Lucía — St. Lucia's
Chapel. This is what remains of the Romanesque cathedral
constructed between 1273 and 1275. The walls are completely
bare and the entrance severe. Inside, the roof is barrel-vaulted
and the walls polished stone, the only additions being the sar-
cophagi on each side, one of Bishop Arnau de Gurb, founder

of the chapel, and the other of Canon Santa Coloma; at the back is the altar, with an image of the Saint, and a little door. It is through here that we recommend the visit to the Cathedral should begin, entering through the cloister. The one we are going to visit is the third of Barcelona's Cathedrals. The first was already in existence in the year 559 when a council was held in the Seo de Barcelona. This was destroyed by Almanzor in 985, and nothing now remains of it. Construction of the second was begun in 1046, and it was finished and consecrated in 1058. All that remains of this one are the few but valuable Romanesque traces to be found in the present, that is the third, Cathedral. This was begun in 1298, as testified by a stone

The Archdeacon's House, today Archivo Histórico of the city

beside St. Ivo's Door in the calle de los Condes. The work continued, with various alterations, until 1422, when it was interrupted. The additions and subsequent reforms do not equal the richness of the orginal building. Among the most recent parts of the construction is the main façade which was begun in 1887 by the architects Mestres and Font who based their design very loosely on the plans drawn up by the French architect Mestre Carli, who had been commissioned in 1408 by the Barcelona Council to propare this façade. To return to the cloister, we shall find that not only is it one of the most beautiful Gothic cloisters in existence, but that it is also interesting for the variety and quality of the component parts. In the form of a quadrangle, it has a portico with slender elegant lines, and is surrounded on three sides by chapels of the old guilds. Many of these chapels still have the original wrought iron grills from the 14th and 15th centuries, marvellous examples of the work

Cathedral cloisters. In the background the door of the old Chapter House

Main façade of the cathedral

The little temple with
fountain in the cloister
on Corpus
celebration day

of the Barcelona craftsmen of the period. The wing of the
cloister attached to the church dates from the 14th century;
the other three were finished and officially inaugurated in 1448.
Continuing round to the right after entering, we come to the
door giving access to what was originally the Sala de Cabre-
vación. Then the Sala Capitular, built between 1405 and 1454,
and today the Museo Catedralicio. At the end of this wing
adjoining the church is the door through which we enter the
main building. It differs from the style of the cloisters in that
it is Romanesque. Opposite this door, in the interior angle of
the cloister, we find another of the delightful details typical of
the whole : the elegant little temple with fountain, the ancient
lavatory commonly found in monasteries and canonicates. The
keystone of the vaulting represents St.George and was carved
by Antoni Claperós. The carving on the ribbing and the effigy
of the Law doctors is the work of the sculptors Pere Oller,
father and son. This little temple has become famous as the
setting, during the Corpus holidays each year, of «l'ou com balla»
− «The dancing egg» in Catalan − an egg-shell dancing on top
of the jet of water from the fountain. The white geese in the
pond are said to symbolise the pure virginity of Saint Eulalia,
one of the patron saints of the city. In the side-chapels, beneath
the floor, and let into the walls are many tombs of persons from
Barcelona's history whose names can be read on the stones.
The cloister can also be entered by the door of Santa Eulalia,

giving onto the calle del Obispo. This unfinished door dates from the 15th century, is in flamboyant Gothic style, and is surmounted by an image of Santa Eulalia carved by Antoni Claperós. A third entrance to the cloisters is through the Puerta de la Piedad in the street of the same name. It is particularly beautiful for the richness of its ornamentation. The wooden retable, Flemish low relief, which may be seen in its archivolt, is the work of the German artist Lochner. Of the exterior accesses to the Cathedral itself, outstanding is the Puerta de San Ivo in the calle de los Condes. It dates from the beginning of the 14th century and is one of the purest examples of architectural art of its period due to the harmony of its proportions and the

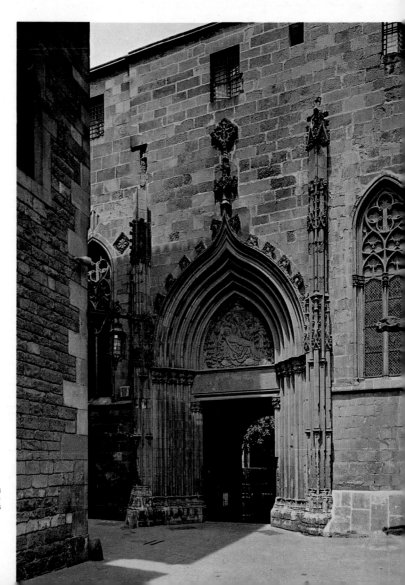

The lovely door «de la Piedad» opening into the Cathedral cloisters

The main façade of the Cathedral strikingly floodlit by night

Aerial view of the
Gothic Quarter
dominated by the great
mass of the Cathedral,
and of a large area of
the city adjoining the port

impeccable refinement of its elements. On entering the Cathedral
through here, we at once find ourselves in the first two sections
of the construction. The upper gallery is divided by double
arching, which was the solution adopted at the beginning of the
construction, and which, had it been continued, would have
given it greater depth. Nevertheless, one is struck at once by
the size of the whole on entering this marvel of Catalan Gothic.
It consists of three high vaulted naves, and though extremely
simple it is not without grandeur. The effect is enhanced by
the enormous pillars and projecting arches. The crossing is just
hinted at at ground level and the flying buttresses are also
reduced to their minimum expression. There are side chapels

between the pillars and the apse is bounded by an aisle with nine more chapels. Over the side chapels there is a gallery running the length of the naves, a characteristic of big cathedrals. Thanks to the genius of its creators, Fabré, Riquer, Roca or Roquer, Solá, Gual and Brugués, the whole construction is notable for its discreet structural simplicity, restrained use of sculpture, ingenious graduation of lighting, and the firm good taste in the distribution of each and every one of the component parts. The staircase to St.Eulalia's crypt leads down from the central nave. This is the work of Jaime Fabré and constitutes a showpiece of Catalan Gothic technique. An extremely low archway forms the entrance; the crypt is covered by almost flat

The Bishop's Street
in the Gothic Quarter

Gothic patio entering the Palacio de la Generalitat, with its staircase supported by a single arch.

vaulting supported by twelve also very shallow arches, the whole converging on a single enormous keystone. Since July 1339 the white marble sarcophagus of Santa Eulalia, an invaluable carving by Nicolás Pissano, has been kept in this crypt. Beside the main altar are the sepulchres of the Catalan monarch Ramón Berenguer and of his wife Almodis, promotors of the 11th century cathedral. The choir, situated in the centre of the building, was begun in 1390 on the initiative of Bishop Ramón de Escales, and one can see his coat-of-arms, consisting of three ladders, sculpted there. The stonework is by the sculptor Jordi Johan, and the wood was begun in 1394 by Pere ça Anglada and finished later by Maciá Bonafé. The stalls are the work of the German master Lochner who has already been mentioned. The coats-of-arms on the seats were carved by Bartolomé Ordóñez and are those of the knights who attended the Capítulo del Toisón de Oro in March 1519 in this choir, convoked by the Emperor Charles Vth. It is impossible to go into more detail about the Cathedral, but it is worth mentioning some of the other things one should note here, such as the Treasure kept in the Sacristy, with King Martin's crown and the ogival monstrance; the retable of Saints Cosme and Damián; the famous 15th century carving, the Lepanto Christ; the retable «La Piedad» in the Museo Catedralicio; the great organ from which hangs the head of a Turk in memory of Ali Babá, decap-

The world-famous Patio de los Naranjos (orange-trees) in the Palacio de la Generalitat.

Palacio de la Generalitat.
Upper gallery
of the Gothic patio.
On the left, entrance to
St. George's Chapel

itated in the Battle of Lepanto; the Bishop's Chair in the presby-
tery; the sepulchres of San Raimundo de Peñafort, of Bishop
Escales — a splendid example of the Gothic style — of Bishop
Ponç de Gualba, of San Olegario — pure Baroque —, the staircase
and balcony of the pulpit, etc. Outside the church again, it is
a good idea to go round to the back of the building to enjoy
a look at the apse with its buttresses, architraves, gargoyles,
windows and the heavy mass of the Campanario de las Horas
— on the other side of the crossing, another belfty of the same
noble style and proportions —, all solidly and firmly constructed
but with careful calculation from the foundations upwards. We
really believe that this view of Barcelona's Cathedral from the
little square behind the apse is esssential to give one the true
feel of the strict religious atmosphere of medieval Barcelona.
A stroll down the calle de los Condes afterwards will complete
the effect, for here there is, first, the Archivo de la Corona de
Aragón; then the Casa de la Inquisición; afterwards the entrance
and steps leading down to the excavations which have revealed
remains of Visigoth houses and a church much older than the
buildings above them; further on, the Museo Marés building
— outstanding among its extensive and valuable contents are
some Hellenic sculptures and carvings of different periods —
and, forming the separation from the Bajada de la Canonja

street, the Casa de la Pía Almoina, one of the oldest and best-conserved buildings in this Barrio Gótico. Back in the little square behind the Cathedral apse and on the other side, is the 14th century Casa de los Canónigos, which was recently restored and also has a façade in the calle del Obispo. The calle del Paradís also leads off this little square, and in this street we shall have the opportunity of visiting the medieval building which is now the home of the «Centre Excursionista de Catalunya». In one of its patios are the columns from the Temple of Augustus built by the Romans on the highest point of the old Barcelona. The point is marked by a millstone let into the surface of the calle del Paradís immediately opposite the excursionist centre, in other words, right on the top of the Mons Taber. From the calle del Paradís we come out into the Plaza San Jaime, where we find, right in front of us, the Palacio de la Generalitat. It is important to realise that the façade of this Palace giving onto San Jaime Square is of much later construction than the most important part of the building; it was added in 1596. It is in Renaissance style and is the work of Pere Blay. The statue

St. George's Salon
in the Palacio de la
Generalitat.

of St. George on horseback is by Andrés Aleu and was placed in its position on the central balcony in 1844. Much more important in all aspects is the Gothic façade giving onto the Calle del Obispo, an outstanding example of the technical mastery and good taste of the architect Marc Çafontand the sculptor Pere Johan who is responsible for the medallion bearing St. George's image and the other sculptures adorning the portal. Outstanding in this ornamental part is the openwork, the gargoyles, and the series of little heads forming a high frieze, all of exceptional realism and beauty. After this marvellous entrance we come to the rear façade, which is in very simple Baroque style and which features a bridge over the street. This was constructed in 1927 and its author, Juan Rubió, intended it to be a summary of the essence of Gothic art. It serves to communicate with the houses on the other side, which also form part of this Gothic Quarter. On going in through the old entrance of the Palacio de la Generalitat, we find ourselves first in the original Gothic patio which is exceptionally beautiful. Prototype of the patios of the great houses of old Cataluña, it has all the balanced loveliness of the best constructions of the epoch. The vestibule has flat vaulting, and the architect has boldly supported delicately decorated the staircase. How marvellous this patio is, becomes even more obvious when we go up to the upper gallery, which has been called the most beautiful in the world. The patio was constructed in 1425 by Marc Çafont, who has been mentioned previously. It is noteworthy that we enter the upper gallery beneath a double arch with suspended capitel unsupported by columns. This was a caprice of the Andalusian artist Gil Medina. The first thing we see in front of us is St. George's Chapel constructed in 1432, also by Marc Çafont. The miniature entrance portal is not without florid Gothic influence. Within, we find that it is small, square, with complicated vaulting,

The historic and artistically outstanding **Salón de Ciento** (Council of One Hundred Chamber) where the Parliament of a Hundred Jurors of the City sat from the 13th to the 15th centuries

The Salón de las Crónicas, with paintings by José M. Sert, in the Casa de la Ciudad or City Council

and richly decorated. Outstanding in this sumptuousness are the carved joints of the arches of the vaulting, the corner tables and works of art from the 14th, 15th and 16 centuries. The image of the Saint is the work of the silversmith Bravo de Seravia, from Soria. Through another side door off the gallery we enter one of the most enchanting spots in Barcelona : the world-famous Patio de los Naranjos. It was constructed between 1526 and 1600 so that it represents a demonstration of the transition from the Gothic to the Renaissance style. The little statue of S.George on top of the small fountain is attributed to Benvenuto Cellini. The loggias, with their Corinthian columns, open on one side, are the work of the already-mentioned Gil Medina; and the paintings in one of them are by Joaquim Mir. Through a door at the end of this patio we enter the sumptuous «Salón de Sesiones» of the "la Generalitat", known as the Cámara Dorada, magnificently decorated by the sculptor Johan de Torres, and with portraits of Catalan kings painted by Ariosto, as well as some tapestries from the superb collection of the old «Audiencia» which had its seat in this building many years ago. The centre of the "La Generalitat de Catalunya" is occupied by the great St. George's Salon, constructed by Pere Blay in 1596. To cover its extensive walls and ceilings the decoration was entrusted to

Fiestas of the Merced, joint patron saint o
the city. The «castellers» forming one of thei
daring, traditional human «towers» in front o
the Casa de la Ciudad or Ayuntamiento
(City Council

the Uruguayan painter Torres-García in 1912. For political
reasons he had to leave his work unfinished so that between
1924 and 1927 his five or six frescos were covered over with
paintings of historical themes by Jorge Mongrell. These latter
are what one now sees on all the walls of the Salon. Leaving
the building by the main steps to St Jaime Square, we see two
bronze lions and a Great Dane by the sculptor Vallmitjana. The
entrance door here is very fine, ornamented with iron, and was
designed by the architect Oliveras. As every visitor discovers, there
is a Guard in the Palacio de la "Generalitat" for protection purposes. It is composed of members of the Cuerpo de "Mossos d'Es-
cuadra" de Cataluña, wearing their traditional uniforms. This body
was founded at the end of the 17th century and is the oldest ins-
titution in Europe with Police functions. On the other side of San
Jaime square is another originally Gothic building which also features a façade added many years later. This is the building of the
Ayuntamiento or Casas Consistoriales, also called Casa de la Ciudad. It corresponds to the English Town Council Hall. As we have
said, the façade was added on to the old construction, and this
was between 1832 and 1836, under the direction of the architect José Mas, and is in neoclassical style. In niches to the left
and right respectively of the entrance are statues of King James
1st and Conseller Fivaller. They were both carved by José Bover
in 1844. Before going into the building it is worth taking a look
at the original entrance which one can find going down the calle
de la Ciudad on the left-hand side of the Ayuntamiento. This façade, infinitely superior to the principal one, is a real architectural
marvel. Gothic in style, it was constructed towards the end of the
14th century, and gives one a very good idea of why is authors, the
sculptor Jordi Johan and the architect Arnau Bargués, enjoyed
such prestige. Over the round arch of the entrance there is an elegant archivolt in the spandrel of which is a relief image of King
David; over this same entrance, three shields with the coats of
arms of Barcelona and Cataluña and an image of the archangel St
Raphael to top it off. Three windows with stone tracery and a second door serve to finish off the gracefulness of the façade rather
than having any definite purpose. Ojival curves, a cornice and
a balustrade with openwork ,tracery and pinnacles finish off
the decoration. Of much more recent epochs are the sculpted
images of St.Eulalia and St.Severo, both beneath canopies and
at the two corners of the frontis. The first is by the sculptor
Flotats (born 1847, died 1897); the second is the work of an
unknown artist. Once inside the building, it is worth seeking
out among the modern installations on the ground floor, the

old Gothic rooms of the «Antic Trentenari» and of the «Trentenari Nou». But the most important part of the building is the great «Salón de Ciento», which the Council of One Hundred Jurors of the City had constructed in the second half of the 14th century. It is on the first floor, the «planta noble». To go to it we can use the black marble staircase on the left, another addition to the old building. It was constructed in 1929, and on the wall beside it are paintings by Miguel Viladric. The sculpture at the top of the staircase represents «Welcome» and was chiselled by Viladomat in 1930. On the right-hand side there is another staircase, the «Escalera de Honor» leading up to the same floor. It is the work of the architects Florensa, Vilaseca and Folguera and is adorned with murals by José M.

General view of the rear façade of Santa Agueda's Chapel built on top of the old walls, and the Cathedral belfries

Sert which have themes concerning the diffusion of culture by
books. On the lower landing there is a bronze statue by José
Llimona representing St.George, standing. On reaching the upper
floor, or planta noble, we find ourselves in a magnificent Gothic
gallery, finished in 1577, as testified by the date carved on one
of the columns. In the same gallery is the door, constructed in
1580, which opens onto the celebrated Salón de Ciento. Here
the hundred «consellers» of the ancient parliament deliberated.
Their executive power was represented by the members of the
«Trentenari Antic i Nou». Pere Llobet began construction of the
Salón in 1369 and the first session was celebrated there on the

Another view from Vía Layetana of the Roman walls, Santa Agueda's Chapel, and the Cathedral belfry towers as they appear when floodlit by night

17th August 1373, an act which was commemorated by placing a stone, which may still be seen, beside the entrance door. At the beginning there were only three arches; but in 1848 two more were added, giving the Salón its present rectangular shape. An alabaster retable dominates the Salón, and in the chairs and in the mosaic of the flooring are the emblems of the different guilds represented in the Consejo de Ciento. Both retable and emblems date from 1925 and are the work of the artists Enrique Monserdá and Antonio Parera. Through a door on the right one enters the adjoining «Salón de Sesiones de la Reina Regente», named after the Queen-Regent because of the portrait of Queen

Maria Cristina with Alfonso 13th as a child, painted by Federico Masriera. The salon is semicircular in form. It was constructed in 1860 to the plans of Francisco Daniel y Molina. The ceiling decoration is the work of the artist Andrés Aleu. The present-day Municipal Council has its meetings here. In other parts, also neoclassical, of the same floor, we find the salones de la Alcaldía (Mayor's Rooms), decorated by Xavier Nogués; the Central or Charles 2nd's salon, with paintings by Ramón Pey; the salon of the Consulado de Mar, so-called in honour of the first assemblage of maritime regulations in Europe (it was written in Catalan with the title «Consolat de Mar») and decorated by Evaristo Mora; the «Salón del Buen Gobierno», with decoration by Josep Obiols; that of the Virgen del Pilar, with unfinished paintings by Ricardo Canals; and of Don Quijote, with paintings by Francesc Galí and J. Martí; and that «Del Trabajo», decorated with frescos by Ramón Rogent. The artists Vila Arrufat and Antonio Tapias have decorated other rooms in this Council Palace. To the left of the Salón de Ciento is the so-called Salón de las Crónicas, a sumptuous and vast room constructed in 1929 and with decoration which is regarded as José M. Sert's masterpiece. It consists of murals, mainly of auriferous material, in which the artist depicts some of the exploits of Catalan and Aragonese sailors in the Orient, under Roger de Flor. Not far

Columns of the Temple of Augustus erected by the Romans in the place which is today the «Centre Excursionista de Catalunya»

from the Ayuntamiento we can visit the church «de los Santos Justo y Pastor». This is a Gothic building dating from 1345 with the celebrated altar of St.Felix, famous for having conserved through the centuries the privilege of the «Testamento Sacramental». According to this privilege, a sworn declaration before two witnesses made in front of this altar has notarial instrument status. Before leaving this old quarter we still have to see the Plaza del Rey, King's Square, a jewel of Gothic art and the scene of innumerable events in the history of Barcelona. Whether we enter from the little square behind the Cathedral or by the calle de Santa Clara, the first building is the Archivo de la Corona de Aragón, formerly Palacio del Lugarteniente, constr-

Main entrance to the old Palacio Real Mayor in the Plaza del Rey

ucted in 1549 under the direction of Antonio Carbonell. It is in Renaissance style with simple lines. One can enter it either from the Plaza del Rey or the calle de los Condes, finding oneself immediately in a very fine patio of two storeys from which the richly-panelled principal staircase leads off. In this Archive there are many old documents of incalculable historical value from all the territories which formed part of the old Catalan-Aragonese kingdom. Opposite the Plaza del Rey entrance is the Casa Padellás, built in the 16th century and today used as the Museo de Historia de la Ciudad. This museum, interesting enough in itself, has the peculiarity that in its cellars one can see traces of the city which existed here in the pre-Christian era. On the same side of the Plaza there is also the Capilla de Santa Agueda (St.Agueda's Chapel) constructed in 1302 to the orders of King James 2nd and his wife Blanca de Anjou. Their coats-of-arms are featured in the decoration of the church. Built over a section of the Roman wall, its special features include the panelled roofing over the nave, which has a double slope, over slender and graceful walls, and its octagonal belfry. Inside is kept the famous retable of the Epiphany by Jaume Huguet, the celebrated 15th century Catalan painter. It was painted by command of the Constable Pedro of Portugal, Pretender to the Catalan-Aragonese throne. The chapel is an annexe to the Palacio Real Mayor which occupies two sides of the Plaza del Rey. This palace was originally built during the period of Romanesque art on the site of the Visigoth cemetery, and various additions were made to it until it reached its present form towards the end of the 14th century. Notable features of the façade include the openwork of the rose-windows and the double-column window-openings. Most of the interior is taken up by the

Entrance of the old Palacio Berenguer de Aguilar in the calle de Montcada, which today contains the famous Picasso Museum, full of visitors throughout the year

Patio of the Palacio of the Marquesses of Lió, also in Barcelona's renowned Montcada street

impressive Salón del Tinell. This was constructed by Guillem Carbonell by command of Peter the Great in 1359, being reformed by Peter 3rd in 1370. It is 35 metres long, 18m. wide and 12m. high, gracefully proportioned under six round arches resting on polygonal pillars, with the ceiling panelled in wood; an unusual construction which makes it one of the loveliest and finest ceremonial halls in the world. On the walls of one of the adjoining rooms were found some murals depicting war exploits of King Peter the Great, in the 13th century. These paintings are now in the Museo de Historia de la Ciudad. Rising up above the Palacio Real Mayor and forming the most ummistakable and typical aspect of the Plaza del Rey is the Mirador del Rey Martín — King Martin's Look-out Tower — a six-storey tower with

Santa María del Mar, one of
the loveliest and most
characteristic constructions in
the severe Catalan
Gothic style

porticoed galleries, constructed in 1555 by Antoni Carbonell. There is a tradition that on the 3rd April 1493, the Catholic Monarchs Ferdinand and Isabel received Christopher Columbus on his return from his first voyage to America in this same Plaza del Rey. Although there is no documentary evidence to support this tradition, it is certainly true that Joan de Canyamás, leader of some rebels from Rheims, attempted to assasinate King Ferdinand the Catholic in December 1492 as the monarch was about to enter the Palacio Mayor. To finish off our look at this part of the city, it is a good idea to leave the Plaza del Rey by the calle de la Llibreteria and go to the Plaza de Berenguer el Grande in Vía Layetana. From here we get a striking view of the other façade of St.Agueda's Chapel rising up above the old walls, with its slender belfry, behind which we can see the Mirador del Rey Martín and the majestic belfry de las Horas of the Cathedral itself. Adjoining the chapel and also constructed

Entrance and main staircase of the Palacio Dalmases, another of the important buildings which have made the calle de Montcada so famous from the historical-artistic point of view

on top of the wall, are other Gothic buildings. In the foreground
is the statue of the Earl-King Berenguer the Great on horseback.
As we shall see, the Vía Layetana is on of the most important
urban thoroughfares, linking as it does, the high part with the
shipping port, passing through the old quarter in the process.
It is a street in which there are many Banks, shipping companies,
insurance companies, savings banks and other organisations of
the greatest influence in the industrial and commercial life of
the country. Quite close to the spot where we came out into
Vía Layetana, we can see one of the most interesting archaeological constructions in this street : this is the old Casa del Gremi
dels Velers, today the Colegio de Arte Mayor de la Seda, with
magnificent graffiti on its two façades and in a niche containing
a Virgin sculpted by Juan Enrich in 1763. This building is on
the corner of the calle Alta de San Pedro, where, a few yards
further down, we find the Palacio de la Música Catalana. This
was inaugurated in 1908 and is the home of the famous «Orfeó
Catalá» as well as being the setting for the most important
concerts in the city. It is the work of the Modernist Catalan
architect Doménech y Muntaner and has aroused both favour-
able and adverse comment. Today however it is regarded as
one of the loveliest surviving examples of fin-de-siecle art. The
sculptured group on the corner symbolises the popular song
and is the work of the artist Miguel Blay. At the other end of

the same street, Alta de San Pedro, is the oldest Christian church in the city. This is Sant Pere de les Puelles, the foundations of which belonged to a church constructed in the epoch of Charlemagne and dedicated to St. Saturnino. Backing onto this part is a church erected for the Conde Sunyer — who died in 950 — dedicated to St. Peter. Additions in Gothic style have been made subsequently. Returning to Vía Layetana, we continue down towards the sea. This will give us the opportunity of looking at large sections of the Roman walls on the right-hand side. These and other remains previously described serve to remind the visitor that when the Romans founded their colony here called Favencia Julia, Augusta, Pía Barcino in the first century B.C., they not only gave it the name in which «Barcelona» has its origin, but they also laid the foundations of an important town, the historical beginnings of the present-day city. At the end of Vía Layetana we find ouselves in the plaza de Antonio López, with its monument put up in 1884 in memory of the dignitary whose name the square bears. This monument is the work of Venancio Vallmitjana. In this square we find the Post Office — the casa de Correos y Telégrafos or Palacio de Telecomunicaciones, constructed by Torres y Goday, with sculptures by Fuixá and paintings inside by Labarta, Obiols, Galí and Canyeles.

The «Dama del Paraguas» (Lady with Umbrella) an excellent souvenir of the Barcelona of the eighties, which has become a symbol of the Barcelona of today. It is in the Parque de la Ciudadela

The Catalonian Parliament in the ''Parque de la Ciudadela' The old Plaza de Armas, with the gardens planned by the Frenchman Forestier; in the centre of the pond, the statue «Desconsol» by the artist Josep Llimona.

Between here and the plaza Palacio is the Casa Lonja de Mar (Maritime Exchange Market), constructed when Barcelona was at its height as a maritime commercial power, that is between 1380 and 1390, so that it is thus the oldest exchange market in the country. All that is left of it today is the Sala de Contrataciones de Bolsa. It is a hall with six arches and «enteixinat» polychrome, of the purest Gothic style and Renaissance Catalan, and is the most notable part of the building. It was constructed by Pere Cabadía. There is also a beautiful patio, of a later epoch, with marble statues and a magnificent staircase leading to the upper rooms which now house the Chamber of Commerce and of Navigation. Most of the neoclassical additions to the original buildings are based on projects of Juan Soler Faneca. Going up Vía Layetana again, we come to the calle de la Princesa from which we enter the famous calle de Montcada. This begins where one finds the capilla (chapel) de Marcús, constructed in 1116 and restored in 1860. It conserves its Romanesque façade. It was the seat of the Cofradía de Carteros (Postmen's Guild). But besides this architectural curiosity there are many others, some more interesting, which have given such extraordinary renown to the calle Montcada. Originally it was called Vía Nova, in the days when it was just a track bordering a sandy watercourse. This was in 1153 when permission was given to Guillermo Ramón de Montcada (perhaps this is the origin of the later name of the street) to build his palace on this spot outside the limits of the city walls. Other palaces were soon erected there, so that the street came to be the most distinguished in Barcelona between the 13th and 18th centuries. But during the 19th century it gradually lost status as its inhabitants abandoned their homes there to go and live in other parts of the city they considered more appropriate for their social position. Today much has been done to restore the old buildings left standing, to rapair the ravages of time, decay and tasteless transformations. The fine house bearing the number 1 dates from the 16th century and was inhabited by Josep Puiguriguer in 1762. Number 12, constructed in the 14th century and restored in the 16th, is the Palacio del Marqués de Lió : it is today the property of the City Council and contains the Museo del Vestido (Dress Museum) which the distinguished citizen Manuel Rocamora handed over as a very important gift to the city in 1961. Number 15 is the Palacio Berenguer de Aguilar, a 13th century work which was successively the residence of the Llinás family and of the Condes de Coloma. Baroque and Renaissance additions have been made to its original Gothic style. Now the property of the City Council, it is the building − interesting enough on its own merits − most visited in Barcelona, because it houses the Picasso

Museum. The original basis for this museum consisted of a donation to the city made by Pablo Picasso's great friend Jaime Sabartés and paintings previously kept in Barcelona's Museum of Modern Art. But not long ago the value of the museum was enormously increased by a very generous gift from the painter himself of over 200 oil paintings, thousands of sketches, notes, finished drawings, water-colours, pastels and engravings. With the previous contents plus this recent renewed demonstration by Picasso of the affection he feels for Barcelona, the visitor to this museum can acquire an irreplaceable basis for getting to know the evolution of the ever-changing Picassian production, from its earliest stages when he was an infant prodigy up to the contemporary period of this forceful nonagenarian creator. And all of this through many of his most important works created with the wide variety of media he has utilised with equal facility. The collection held in the Picasso Museum was enlarged so much that it was necessary to utilise the Palacio del barón de Castellet, a 17th century construction adjoining the Palacio Berenguer de Aguilar, to accommodate the additions. So that there is no doubt whatsoever that Barcelona has the most complete collection in the world of the artistic works of Pablo Picasso. Continuing along calle Montcada, we come to

number 20, the Palacio de los Dalmases. Although it has deteriorated over the years, it is still a valuable component in this rich collection of old buildings. Constructed in the 17th century as the residence of Pablo Ignacio Dalmases, it was later the seat of the constitution of the «Academia dels Desconfiats», and during the War of Succession it was occupied by the «Veinticuatrena de Guerra». Number 21 is a large, plain house, also of the 17th century but in bad repair. The following one, number 23, is older (14th century) but retains only a few fine traces of the original construction. It is said that the original palace of the Montcadas stood on the site now occupied by house number 25. The palace was later occupied by the «Diputació dels Estaments de Catalunya», and subsequently became the property of a Genoan family called Giudice at the beginning of the 17th century. The Giudices were involved in revolutionary movements of various kinds, to the point of provoking a popular rising in 1624, in the course of which the palace was burnt and destroyed. The present building was constructed in the second half of the 17th century and is known as the palacio de los Cervelló after the family who lived there. At the end of the calle Montcada we find one of the most valuable surviving examples of Gothic art : the church Basílica de Santa María del Mar, archetype of Catalan medieval architecture. The famous French historian Pierre Lavedan has written of it : «It is the most beautiful victory of mind over matter witnessed by the Middle Ages». And it certainly has aroused great admiration throughout the world. Its façade is at the same time sumptuous and delicate, with a main entrance featuring numerous concentric archevolts, the well-balanced windows, the extraordinary proportions of the belfry, the main body of the construction, the door of the apse, and other external parts are all artistic marvels; and inside

Barcelona Zoo in the Parque de la Ciudadela. One of the skilful dolphins performing its tricks

Various examples of the African fauna in the Barcelona Zoo

the enormous height allows one to admire the purity of style and the complete unity rare in Gothic constructions. This unity is due to the fact that the whole building was completed between 1329 and 1383, during the reign of Peter 3rd, when the last keystone of the vaulting was put into place. As well as the singular features already referred to, we must draw attention to the architecture of the interior : the enormous and very high vaulting is supported on remarkably few columns which are thus separated from each other by 13 metres, the widest known separation for such cases. Apart from the old retable by Bernat Carbonell, Deodat Casanovas's main altar and the sculptures by the celebrated artist Gurri are worthy of attention. Back at the bottom of Vía Layetana again, we have the Paseo de Colón on our right, an important traffic artery with the attractive feature

View of one of the
sectors of African
animals in the same zoo

of a magnificent perspective over the shipping harbour. What
was for centuries the sea-wall is today a busy avenue which
conserves, however, the original maritime atmosphere. On the
built-up side, the first construction of interest is the house bearing
the number 6. It was constructed in the 16th century though
it has been subjected to unfortunate reformations. Its interest
stems from the fact that Miguel de Cervantes, author of Don
Quijote, is claimed to have stayed there when he visited Barcelona. Further on, the most outstanding building is the Capitanía
General, on the site of a Convent of the Order of the Merced
of which the lovely stone and marble patio inside is a relic. The
façade was restored by the architect Adolfo Florensa in 1928.
Behind the Capitanía General is the church Basílica de la Merced,
built between 1765 and 1775 to the plans of Josep Mas. Both
the façade and the cupola bear witness to the good taste and
talent of the architect. The sculpture is by Carlos Grau. Inside,
the altar is the work of Vicens Marro, and there is a very valuable
polychromed carving of the Virgen de la Merced, joint patron
saint of Barcelona, attributed to Pere Moragues and dating from
the 14th century. Although of Baroque style, the church has a
Gothic entrance which was taken from the demolished church
of San Miguel close to the Casas Consistoriales. Returning to
the Paseo de Colón, we soon reach the beautiful Plaza de
Medinaceli. Here there is the fine monument to Admiral Galcerán
Marquet by the celebrated architect Daniel y Molina. The statue
of the admiral was sculpted by Santigosa Vestratem. This
monument was finished in 1851 and is 18 metres high. Now
we must move on to the Plaza de Palacio, nerve-centre of the
city from time immemorial. One or the principal buildings in it
is the Lonja de Mar, described above. On the other side, along
the Paseo de Isabel II and on the corner of the square itself
is the block of porticoed houses commonly known as «els
portics d'En Xifré» which were built in 1836 for a citizen of that
name who had made his fortune in the shipping trade. The
noteworthy low-reliefs decorating the façades are the work of
the artists Campeny, Doménec and Padró. On the opposite

corner is the Palacio del Gobierno Civil, the construction of which was begun in 1790 to the plans of the Andalusian Conde de Roncali. It is in neoclessical style and has three magnificent façades and an ornate central patio. Closing off the square and with its back to the Barceloneta and the sea is the Escuela Oficial de Náutica, constructed by Adolfo Florensa between 1927 and 1929. The centre is occupied by an old monumental fountain made by the Italian Baratta de Leopoldo brothers to the plans of the oft-mentioned Daniel y Molina. The fountain is crowned by a winged figure symbolising Catalan genius; below it, four seated statues represent the four provinces into which Cataluña is divided, and in the basin, four fountains symbolise the rivers Llobregat, Ebro, Ter and Segre. It was erected as a tribute to General Campo Sagrado for his work in bringing water from Montcada to Barcelona, and was inaug-

Examples of African fauna in the richly varied collection of all kinds of animals to be found in the Barcelona Zoo

urated in 1856. Leaving the Plaza del Palacio behind us, we pass the R.E.N.F.E. railway station known as Estación de Francia and come to the Parque de la Ciudadela. This park, laid out in its present form at the end of last century, occupies the site of the enormous fortress of the Ciudadela built between 1715 and 1718, more to maintain an iron vigilance over the city which had just been conquered through the War of Succession, than to defend it. For its construction it was necessary to tear down the 800 houses of the district known as the Ribera. It wasn't until 1869 that the State gave to Barcelona City Council «the site of the destroyed fortress of the Ciudadela». Four years later the Council converted this enormous site into a public park following the plan presented by José Fontseré. In this plan, the fruit of which was the present Parque de la Ciudadela, Fontseré was helped by the architect José Vilaseca, and, as from 1877, by a young student who was later to become world-famous : Antonio Gaudí. The Universal Exhibition of 1888 gave opportunity and incentive to enlarge and enrich the park with the incorporation of fountains, palaces, monuments and new gardens. Quite recently more improvements have been made, under the direction of Ramón Oliva. Many exotic plants have been introduced. The basic framework of the park is provided by three principal avenues called respectively «de los álamos» (poplars), «de los olmos» (elms), and «de los tilos» (limes). A large lake gives the beauty and distinction water always confers on gardens. The most spectacular monument in the Parque de la Ciudadela is the Cascada Monumental, not very far from the lake. It is in neoclassical style and is the work of José Fontseré and Antonio Gaudí. The statues are by Venancio

Flamingoes and pelicans
in the Parque Zoológico

The white-haired gorilla
«Copito de Nieve»
(Snowflake), considered
unique of its kind, and
one of the most admired
animals in the
Barcelona Zoo

Vallmitjana and the Cuadriga de la Aurora right at the top, in bronze, is by Rosendo Nobás. On the other side of the lake is the plaza de Armas. Surrounded by an attractive garden and a pond, in the centre of this square, is Josep Llimona's nude statue «Desconsol». On one side of this square are the buildings of the Palacio del Gobernador and of the Capilla de la Ciudadela, built by Verboom in 1748; opposite is what was originally the Arsenal de la Ciudadela and is today, considerably enlarged, the Catalonian Parliament. The original part of this building was the work of the engineers Verboom and Retz, who were also responsible for the fortress in 1714. In the museum one can admire paintings by Fortuny, Rusiñol, Mir, Casas, Nonell, Zuloaga, and Solana, and sculptures by Llimona, Clará, Gargallo, Viladomat, Clarassó, Hugué and Rebull. One can also find here

The great «Cascada» of the Parque de la Ciudadela, designed by the architects Antonio Gaudí and José Fontseré

the Galería de Numismática and the Galería de Catalanes Ilustres. Among the many works of art distributed through the gardens, it is worth mentioning the mounted statue of General Prim, an exact copy made by Federico Marés of an earlier one on the same spot by Puigjaner; the monument to the Voluntarios Catalanes in the 1914-18 war, by Josep Clará; and the «Dama del Paraguas», sculpted in 1888 by Roig y Soler, which has since become an amusing and romantic symbol of the city of Barcelona. This latter sculpture surmounts the two basins of a gracefully elegant fountain now within the boundaries of the Zoological Park. This zoo, always crowded with visitors, both local and from all over the world, is one of the most interesting features of Barcelona. Within the magnificent setting of the Parque de la Ciudadela, it is, because of the modernity and efficient maintenance of its installations, one of the five best in Europe. Animals of all kinds and varieties are together here under conditions which, while preserving the atmosphere of the Park in which the Zoo is set, are also made to correspond as nearly as possible to those appropriate for each animal. Water and vegetation have been intelligently employed to give a

"Arco de Triunfo" seen from
"Paseo de San Juan".

"Arco de
Triunfo"
this was the
main entrance
to the Universal
Exhibition held in
Barcelona in 1888.

certain degree of liberty to each class of animal. The person
responsible for all of this has been Antonio Jonch, present
Director of this extraordinary Zoo. On a flowerbed beside one
of the entrances there is a statue of St. Francis of Assisi, the
work of Pedro Jou, reminding visitors of the loving-kindness
they should show to animals. There is also a group of statuary
comprising a monument to Walt Disney, that famous cartoonist
whose popular animals became celebrated personalities in his
films. It consists of several bronze gazelles and is the work of
Nuria Tortras. Over all, there are a hundred and sixty installations
in the Zoo, including lawns, patios, ponds, cages, etc., in which
the different animals can move around, some of them in apparent
liberty − for example the white gorila «Copito de Nieve», Snow-

The centre of the Plaza de Cataluña,
nerve-centre of this great town

flake, and the trained dolphins with their circus-like exercises in
the marvellous pool within the no less important Aquarium.
Before leaving the Parque de la Ciudadela, we can still visit
the Museo Martorell, a museum of petrography, mineralogy and
paleontology; and the Museo de Historia Natural installed in
the redbrick building which looks like a medieval castle with
battlements and coats-of-arms at one end of the Paseo de los
Tilos. It was designed by Doménech y Muntaner. Near this
museum the delightful little fountain by Reynés shows a perfect
combination of realism and artistic beauty in its sculptures of
children playing together. Leaving the Park by the gateway
giving access to the Passeig Lluís Companys, we see in front
of us the monument to Rius y Taulet, Mayor of Barcelona and
promoter of the 1888 Exhibition as well as of a great number
of urban reforms. The monument is the work of the architect
Pedro Falqués, with sculptures by Manuel Fuxá, and was finished in 1901. Continuing up the same Paseo, we find the enormous mass of the Palacio de Justicia on our right. It was finished
in 1911 and was planned by the architects Sagnier, Doménech
and Estapé in a personal re-interpretation of neoclassical style.

Calle de Urgel

Uni

Plaza
Universidad

Plaza de
Cataluña

Parque Güell

Av. República Argentina

Calle Balmes

Calle de la

Calle Mayor de Gracia

Placa
ancesc
Maciá

Avinguda

Calle

de la

Gracia

Calle de la Travesera de Dalt

C. Larrard

Calle Escorial

Plaza
Sanllehí

Travesera

Carrer Pi I Margall

de Gracia

Casa Milá
(La Pedrera)

Calle Balmes

Casa Batlló
Casa Amatller

Via Layetana

Casa Lleó

Passeig de Sant Joan

Cerdeña

Provenza

de

la

Templo de
la Sagrada
Familia

Avda. Gaudí

Calle

del Consejo

de Ciento

Passeig de Diagonal

C. Marina

Gran Via de les Corts

Paseo

Oficina de
Información
y Turismo

Plaza
Tetuán

Catalànes

Carlos I

Plaza de Toros
Monumental

Plaza Obispo
Urquinaona

Paseo

Autopistas A-17 y A-19

It is 115 metres long and 60 wide. Inside there is a salon of «pasos perdidos» with paintings by José M. Sert. In other rooms one can see most of the collection of magnificent old tapestries which were formely in the Palacio de la Generalitat. At the end of the Passeig Lluís Companys is the Arco de Triunfo which was the principal entrance to the 1888 Exhibition. It was planned and built by José Vilaseca. It has a high frieze sculpted by Llimona, and, in spite of its size is well-proportioned. The designer's attempt to suggest Moorish art by his use of red brick and majolic construction may be considered a success. It is 30 metres high and 27 wide. To round off this itinerary we are going to continue up the Paseo de San Juan, in front of the Arco de Triunfo. A little further up after Plaza de Tetuán we come to the church and convent of the Salesas Reales, of modern Gothic style, built between 1882 and 1885 to the plans of the architect Juan Martorell. Finally, a few metres further on, is the monument to the poet Mosén Cinto Verdaguer, work of the sculptor brothers Miguel and Luciano Oslé, and of Borrell and Nicolau.

For our third itinerary across Barcelona it is a good idea to use Plaza Cataluña as our starting-point again. From here we

Plaza de la Universidad

Paseo de Gracia. The famous block of buildings known as the «manzana de la discordia» because it contains such widely-differing examples of the architecture of the Catalan modernists of the end of the 19th and beginnings of the 20th centuries

shall begin our journey in Paseo de Gracia, entering at once right into the sector of the city known as the Ensanche. This is the name used, since its origins in 1860-1870, for that part of Barcelona which was constructed when the walls were knocked down and the city expanded out to the then villages of Sants, San Gervasio, Sarriá and Les Corts. These are now districts forming the limits of the city which is spreading out beyond the rivers Besós and Llobregat and climbing up the mountains forming its northern limits. Following the plans of the engineer Cerdá, the houses in the Ensanche were built in regular blocks, 100 metres by 100 metres, in streets which were absolutely straight and had an unvarying width of 20 metres – wider ones can be countes on the fingers of one hand –

Plaza de Juan Carlos I, at the top of Paseo de Gracia.

so that the crossings were always at right-angles. There are about sixty streets like this, forming an immense grille which seems to surround the old part of the city on every side except where it is bounded by the sea. So from Plaza Cataluña the physiognomy of the city changes. The first few paces we take up Paseo de Gracia will be sufficient to show us that this is a more modern part. We shall discover many other peculiarities apart from the straightness of the streets. Paseo de Gracia is the widest street − sixty metres − in the new sector, and is the one which separates the Ensanche into two parts, left and right. It is an exceptional street because of its four rows of trees, two pavements, two promenades and three roadways; not to mention the luxuriousness of its shops and the distinction of its fine fin-de-siècle houses, the rich modernism of later constructions and the functional buildings of banking and other economic establishments. And even more striking, it has the distinction

Paseo de Gracia
Façade of «La Pedrera»
showing the genius of
the original architect
Gaudí

Roof and chimneys of «La Pedrera», one of the most original creations of the now world-famous architect Antonio Gaudí. In the background, the spires of the Sagrada Familia, the same artist's most grandiose creation

unique to Barcelona, if not unique in the world, of possessing a block of houses in which the different styles of the most important architects of Modernism are represented. Modernism was in vogue in Cataluña at the end of the last century and the beginning of the present one, and this block of houses, known as the manzana de la discordia, may be seen going up on the left-hand side between Consejo de Ciento and Aragón. Of this

architectural «discordia», the first example is the casa Lleó Morera, number 35, where the original genius of its author, Doménech y Muntaner, gave free rein to his liking for rich ornamentation with floral themes. Further on, house number 39 is in Louis XVI style, but treated with discretion in its modernistic interpretation, as was the custom with its author, Enrique Segnier. Next we find the casa Amatller, number 41, typical of its architect, Puig y Cadafalch, an expert in restyling the elements of northern Gothic and Renaissance Catalan. The next house, number 43, is the casa Batlló, work of Gaudí, and a good example of his very personal interpretation of Modernism, with the cult of the curved line. It is worthy of note that Gaudí used the form of human bones for the configuration of the masses, balconies and columns of this house. The architectural contrasts we have just pointed out become even more evident if we compare the four houses described with those in the block on the other side of the road, and also with many others along

On this and the following page, the Sagrada Familia, masterpiece of the Catalan architect Antonio Gaudí

The church of the Sagrada
Familia. Façade of the
Nativity, planned and built
during the life of its
original creator
Antonio Gaudí

Paseo de Gracia. Such study offers us a complete display of
all the architectural tendencies from the end of the last century
up to the present day. We shall find a invaluable example in
this exhibition of the art of designing and constructing buildings
where the calle Provenza crosses Paseo de Gracia. This is the
famous casa Milá, known all over the world as «La Pedrera»,
another of Gaudí's works, the construction of which was begun
in 1905. In this work Gaudí gives a clear demonstration of the
original plastic vision he was attemting to impose upon architecture, so anticipating aesthetic movements of his own and
later epochs. It is claimed that when Gaudí was asked to justify

the curvilinear volumes of this construction, he replied : «They are explained by their connection with the forms of the mountains surrounding Barcelona, visible from the site of the house». But it has also been said that in his conception of this mass of stone, Gaudí wanted to portray the undulation of waves. Whatever the case may be, it is clear that we have before us an abstract sculpture of monumental proportions where the conditions of unity, plasticity and expressivism have been complied with with surprising mastery. Nobody remains indifferent when he looks at the imposing power of the façade of this house, «La Pedrera», at the Cyclopean effectiveness of its entrance and doors and windows, at the twisted plant-like forms of the ironwork, and

Top of one of the four belfries of the Sagrada Familia, which enables us to appreciate fully the enormous originality of Gaudí's art, and the wide range of colours and forms he used

Aerial view of the "Sagrada Familia".

Detail of the façade of
the Nativity of the
church of the
Sagrada Familia

the fantastic shapes of its roof-line. If we want to see more of
Gaudí's work we can follow calle Provenza off to the right and
after passing the monument to Mosén Cinto Verdaguer, we
come to the templo de la Sagrada Familia, situated between
the streets Provenza and Mallorca and Cerdeña and Marina.
Work on the construction of this church was begun in 1882 by
the architects Martorell and De Villar. It wasn't until 1891 that
Gaudí took over the direction of the project which was to
become the great Barcelona cathedral. His death — he was
knocked down by a tram in one of the city streets on the 7th
June 1926 — prevented him, if not from finishing the work, for
this would be impossible within the life-span of one or even

The park-keeper's lodge in the Parque Güell,
an urbanisation where Gaudí gave free rein to
his original inventive genius, creating fantasies
in combinations of vegetation and stone

Top of the cupola of the
lodge in the Parque Güell,
another example of the striking
solutions adopted in
Gaudí's architecture

two constructors of any of the great cathedrals, at least from
pursuing his task further than he did. When he took over the
management he modified his predecessors' project, imposing
on the new plan his own very personal inventiveness. He finished
the crypt, which was one of the parts already started, but subst-
ituting a more ambitious and more original architectural struct-
uring. In 1893 the apse was finished, still showing signs of
Gothic style. Immediately afterwards the construction of the
completely original Nativity façade was begun. He had planned
it in 1891, but throughout the building it was modified in
accordance with his constant desire to modify his artistic con-
ceptions. By 1925, one of the four spires which now crown this
façade had been added. The other three had only been begun
when Gaudí died in 1926, but they were finished exactly as he
had planned them. What we have described is all that he was
personally able to supervise. Nevertheless, this façade with its
four spires where the great allegory of the Nativity is set out,
is a sufficient indication of the extraordinary significance of
Gaudí's artistic creations. Not only does it represent a radical
innovation in architecture, but it also shows a most surprising
use of the decorative elements. And all of this conceived and
executed with masterly technique, with absolute confidence in
his own ability to defy the problems of desequilibrium and
disharmony. The Sagrada Familia, although unfinished, is the
biggest and most important of Gaudí's productions, which is why
it is studied and admired by people from all over the world.
In accordance with Gaudí's ambitious, intrepid project, the
church of the Sagrada Familia should be considered as an
enormous symbolic edifice. If Gaudí's original plans are resp-

Parque Güell. Part of one of the
avenues supported on sloping columns
of rough stone. As can be seen, this
is one of many original architectural
inventions by Gaudí

Parqué Güell. The great staircase
leading to the Hall of a Hundred Columns

Below, the Hall of a Hundred Columns, covered by the Gran Plaza, bordered by an undulating bench, in the Parque Güell. On the right, the Cross rising up above the keeper's lodge in the same park constructed by Gaudí

ected, the church will have five naves without buttresses, with an apse aisle of hexagonal radial chapels, and ellipsoidal vaulting supported on sloping columns. All the plans of the building will be complicated hyperboloids. The dome above the centre of the crossing will be very high. The cupola above the apse will symbolise the Virgin Mary. The church will have three enormous entrances : the Eastern one, dedicated to the Nativity, is at the right-hand end of the crossing − this is the one already finished with its four spires −; the Western one, dedicated to the Passion and Death of Our Lord, will be at the opposite end of the crossing; and the Southern façade will be that of the Glory and the Resurrection and will be the biggest of all. Each of these entrances will have four spires, like the one already finished. The total of twelve spires will represent the twelves apostles. Four taller spires around the dome will symbolise the four evangelists. These latter four will surround an even higher one − 170 metres − representing the Saviour. To finish off this brief description of the church of the Sagrada Familia we should mention that the author of this extraordinary project, Antonio Gaudí, is buried in the crypt. In continuation we can visit another

production of the same architect, also strikingly original : the Parque Güell, situated beyond the district of Vallcarca or, according to the route chosen, at the end of the street Travesera de Dalt and before entering the district of La Salud. The Parque Güell is the result of a donation made to the city by the Conde de Güell in 1900 with the express condition that Gaudí should take charge of the urbanisation of the land to form a residential colony in the style of the garden-cities then in vogue. Gaudí was authorised to utilise his very personal inventive talent for such constructions and decoration as he thought fit over the 15 hectares of the donation. The project for the residential colony came to nothing, but by 1904 Gaudí had created these

End of the staircase giving access to the «Sala Hipóstila» or Hall of a Hundred Columns in the Parque Güell

gardens for Barcelona, unique in the world. Subsequently he added the great terrace running round the lip of the underground hall, encircling what was intended to be the amphitheatre of a Greek theatre. This was all finished in 1912. The wall of this terrace synthesises the idea of «total art» which Gaudí used throughout the Park. It is something which, while starting off from painting, sculpture and architecture, cannot be contained within the normal limits of any of them. In the trajectory of Gaudí's work, these terrace-walls perhaps represent the final abandoning of historical references and the complete liberation of his enormous creative force in its application to totally original forms. As one can see, it consists of Manises ceramics in different colours and sizes arranged in the form of an enormous collage.

Parque Güell. Section of the undulating bench bordering the Gran Plaza. Gaudí used forms which had never been seen before in its construction

The whites, blues, ochres violets and yellows are arranged in
careful disorder, emphasising the different relief zones. Is this
perhaps a demonstration of what Gaudí meant when he wrote
in his chronicle : «Colour in architecture must be intense, logical
and fecund.» In 1914 work on this Park — truly revolutionary
in its artistic expression — was finally finished. Le Coubusier
write of its author : «Gaudí is the man who has had most architectural creative force among all the men of his generation.» The
visitor to Barcelona should know that scattered through the
city are other examples of Gaudí's art. Chronologically, the first
of these has to be Casa Vicens, which is in the street Calle
Carolinas and was built between 1878 and 1880 when Gaudí
was 26 years old, and which allows one to admire the daring
with which the young architect combined masonry and polychromed ceramics; then, the Colegio de Santa Teresa de Jesús,
built in 1889 in the calle de Ganduxer, which is a demontration
of just how much can be done with red brick and parabolic
arches; another interesting construction is the pavilion which
Gaudí put in the finca Güell in Avinguda de Pedralbes, with its
walls and gates which show Moorish influences; then there is
the casa Calvet, built as number 48 calle de Caspe between
1898 and 1899, where Gaudí gives his personal interpretation
of Baroque style while indulging his liking for wrought iron
decoration; and finally we must mention the casa Figueras,
better known as «Bellesguard», another personal interpretation

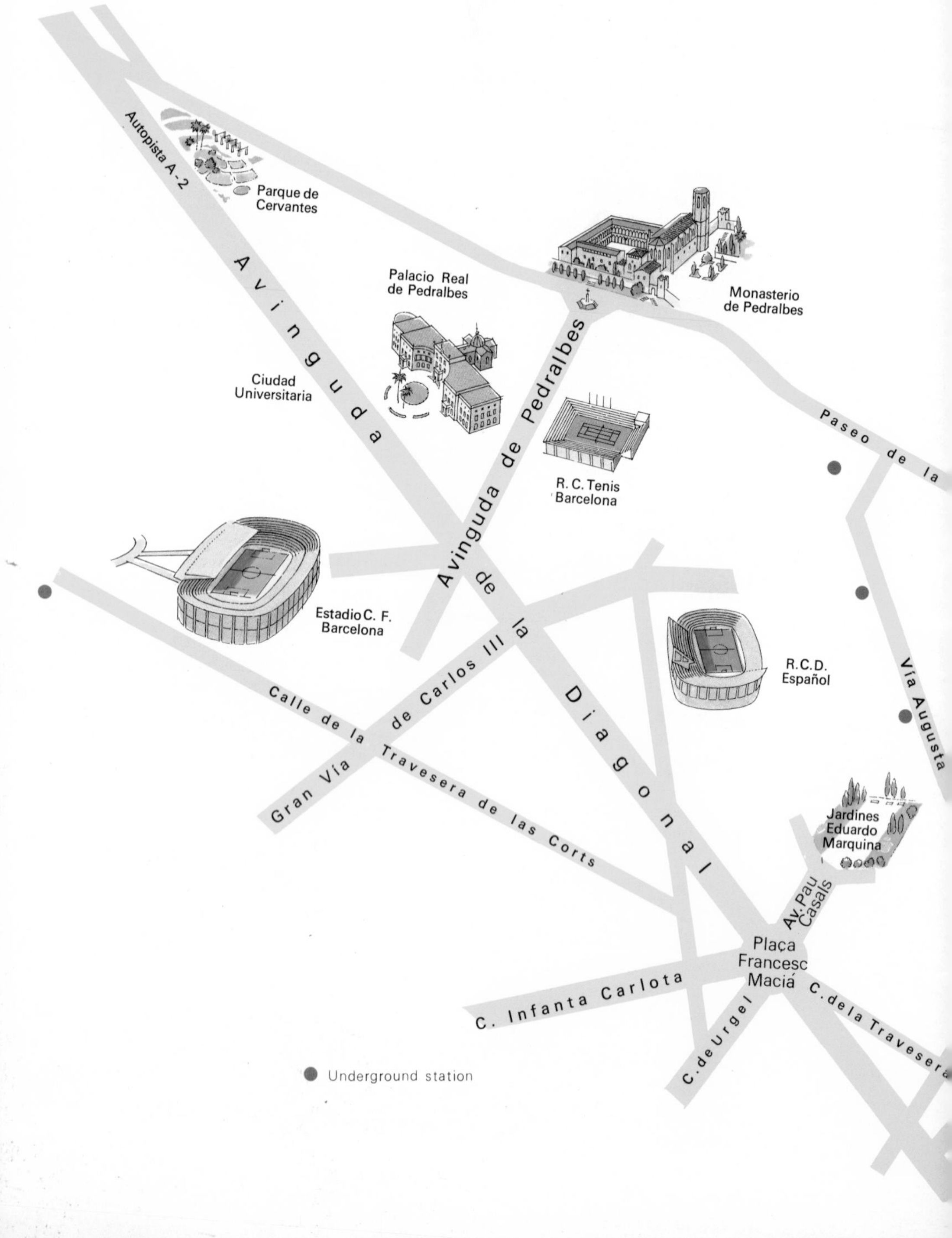

Autopista A-2

Parque de
Cervantes

A v i n g u d a

Palacio Real
de Pedralbes

Monasterio
de Pedralbes

Ciudad
Universitaria

A v i n g u d a   d e   P e d r a l b e s

Paseo   de   la

R. C. Tenis
Barcelona

Estadio C. F.
Barcelona

d e   C a r l o s   I I I

l a

D i a g o n a l

R.C.D.
Español

Via Augusta

Calle de la

Gran Via   T r a v e s e r a   d e   l a s   C o r t s

Jardines
Eduardo
Marquina

Av. Pau Casals

Plaça
Francesc
Maciá

C.de Urgel

C. Infanta   Carlota

C. de la Travesera

● Underground station

Tibidabo

Parque de Atracciones

Funicular al Tibidabo

Observatorio Fabra

Andreu

Av. del Dr.

Carretera

Tibidabo

Av. República Argentina

Calle Balnes

nes de rolas

Calle Mayor de Gracia

On top of the Tibidabo mountain.
The Funfair vantage point and,
in the background, the church
of the Sagrado Corazón

Aerial panorama of the top of the Tibidabo dominated by the church of the Templo Expiatorio del Sagrado Corazón, and set amid extensive woods stretching out to beyond the Vallés and the distant mountains

The top of the Tibidabo mountain

of Gaudí's, but this time of Gothic style. As well as the massive
cross on top of the daringly stender spire, the interior is well
worth study. Gaudí constructed it between 1900 and 1902 on
the ruins of King Martin's summer residence. After visiting the
Sagrada Familia we can return to Paseo de Gracia along the
"Avinguda de la Diagonal" so called because it crosses the Ensanche diagonally. It is really the most important street in Barcelona, both because of its style and its length. After leaving the
monument to Mosén Cinto Verdaguer y Cadafalch's «casa de les
Punxes», on the corner of the Avenida and calle Rosellón. It was
constructed at the beginning of this century and the author suc-
cessfully combined Gothic architecture with the Modernism of the
time. Continuing, we come to the Plaza de Juan Carlos I, known
since its origin as the «Cinc d'Oros», and formed by the crossing
of the two most beatuiful streets in the city, the Paseo de Gracia
and the Avinguda de la Diagonal. The magnificent perspectives
one can see in all four directions from this square are enhanced
by the thick avenues of trees. Apart from the central monument
and the enormous banking establishment on one side, it is worth

looking at the house on the corner opposite the bank mentioned. This building is the Palacio Robert, owned by a commercial firm, and, as one can see, a magnificent example of the best in urban architecture. The good taste of its styling shows French influences. It was constructed in 1901-2 and is the work of the architect Juan Martorell. Unfortunately, in 1951 a tall building was constructed right next to the Palace, dwarfing it to such an extent that much of its original artistic merit has been lost. The continuation of Paseo de Gracia on the other side of Plaza de Juan Carlos I is the Calle Mayor de Gracia, which in its turn leads into the Avenida de la República Argentina. It is worth going right to the top of this latter street to see how the persistent and rapid spread of Barcelona is taking the city up the flanks of the Collcerola range of hills forming its northern horizon. These same hills protect the city from the cold northerly winds. This is also the route to get to one of the places all visitors to Barcelona have to go to – the Tibidabo, highest point of the Collcerola hill range. One gets to the top either by car or after a

Some of the installations in the Funfair on the Tibidabo. In the background the church of the Sagrado Corazón

short journey by bus and funicular railway. More because of its situation than its height (500 metres) the Tibidabo is a marvellous viewpoint for the whole area of greater Barcelona and beyond, to the other sides of the rivers Besós and Llobregat. The city is stretched out at our feet with the wide spread of the Mediterranean beyond it as far as the distant horizon. On either side of us, the marvellous and varied undulations of the hill-tops, La Rabassada, Vallvidrera, San Pedro Mártir, leading on to more distant hills. Looking in the opposite direction, away from the city, the view from the top of the Tibidabo is equally fine, indeed one of the most striking views one could wish for. In the foreground is the enormous green expanse of the woods; to left and right the Levante and Poniente hill ranges respectively, closing off the district of the Vallés which is spread out before us with its multiplicity of countryside scenery. Further away we can see Montserrat, Sant Llorenç del Munt, Sant Miquel del Fay, Montseny and other unusual-shaped mountains. Further away still, especially on clear days, the distant peaks of the Pyrenees. But the Tibidabo has other attractions as well as the view it offers. Half way up to the the top is the Observatorio Fabra and the Museo de Ciencias Físicas, both institutions from the legacy left to the city for these purposes by Camilo Fabra, marqués de Alella, in 1904. Right on the summit of the mountain there is a church, the templo expiatorio del Sagrado Corazón, the work of the architect Enrique Segnier. It is Gothic rather than discreet in style, but not without a certain majestic grandeur. It is worthwhile going up to the high platform of one of the spires by the lift which has been installed for this purpose, to be able to enjoy the complete panoramic view one gets from there. In addition, one can amuse oneself in the Tibidabo's Funfair equipped with a variety of installations for the enjoyment of children, young people and − why not? − adults, too. Spacious terraces, little squares, promenades and delightful gardens surround the great church and the Funfair. And of course, there is no lack of bars, restaurants and hotels. Whichever way we come down from the top, we are sure to find snack-bars and establishments selling drinks and typical meals. As we reach the outside edge of the city on our way down we can stop off and look at the Royal Monastery of Pedralbes, an invaluable part of the rich architectural collection of old Barcelona. It is situated on the upper side of the square formed by the end of Avinguda de Pedralbes and the road Carretera de Esplugues. Founded by Queen Elisenda of Montcada, wife of James 2nd, the Real Monasterio de Pedralbes was begun in 1324 and finished in 1412. It was planned by Guillem d'Abiell and constructed by Ferrer Peiró and Doménec de Granyena. It was

constructed during the best period of Catalan architecture and
the rapidity with which it was finished made its marvellous unity
possible. In 1343, Ferrer Bassa, a disciple of Giotto, painted
St Michael's Chapel, one of the most interesting parts of the
monastery. These murals have particular value when one realises
that they are certainly the only complete works in existence by
this famous artist. One must not fail to take a look at the cloisters:
they are of three storeys and among the most beautiful of their
kind in the Gothic style. Neither should one miss the Sala
Capitular, with its mural paintings also; or the very fine gardens
both interior and exterior. Among the notable sepulchres in the

The church of the Templo
Expiatorio del Sagrado
Corazón at the top of the
Tibidabo. This building
was constructed by the
architect Enrique Sagnier

Monastery, the most outstanding is that of the Queen-founder
with its prone statue sculpted in alabaster. The nave of the
church is impressively majestic, in spite of its extreme simplicity.
The façade is decorated with the coats-of-arms of the Montcadas. One can still see remains of the old protective walls and
two of the small fortified entrance gateways. From this peaceful,
isolated spot we move on into the rush and bustle of the city,
with its traffic and modern buildings. Following the carretera
de Esplugues, we come to the point where it joins the end of
the Avinguda de la Diagonal and where the very modern motorway linking Barcelona with the rest of the country begins. At

this point, the most beautiful entry to Barcelona, an exceptional panorama opens out before us. On one side, the mountains crowning Barcelona; on the other the long, blue band of the Mediterranean fading away into the horizon. And below us, cutting across the plain of the Llobregat river, the new urbanisations comprising the outlying districts of the city. In the background, the great mass of the mountain Montjuïc keeps watch over the city. Where we are standing, the most modern part of this great city reaches out to us, for we are on the dividing line between the city and the surrounding villages now almost absorbed by the great metropolis. And the Avinguda de la Diagonal cuts right across the middle of this, disappearing into a

Another view of the top of the Tibidabo, showing the big, modern Funfair

dim distance where it seems to be cut off by the sea. Once we have had our fill of this magnificent panorama, we must take a look at the Parque Cervantes on our left. Apart from its lay-out and contents, this park has the merit of an area unsurpassed by any of the gardens in the interior of the city. As we go down the Avinguda de la Diagonal we very quickly come to the modern zone of the Ciudad Universitaria. To the right and left of the great avenue are the buildings of the Advanced Mercantile Studies School, the Faculty of Political Science and Economics, the School of Technical Architects, the Higher School of Architecture, St. George's Fine Arts School, the School of Industrial

Engineers, the Faculty of Sciences, the Faculty of Pharmacy, Faculty of Medicine, Faculty of Law, plus the administration buildings and restaurants of the Sports Grounds of the University City. The tall Law Faculty building is outstanding among these. The most modern European techniques were used in its construction, and its Great Hall is specially equipped for all kinds of meetings and congresses, with magnificent mural decorations by the painter Jaume Muxart. Separated from the University City by a large zone of trees and shrubs and on the upper side of the avenue, is the Palacio de Pedralbes. This was constructed between 1919 and 1925 to plans by the architects Borrás and Nebot. A donation made to King Alfonso 13th by some impor-

The Rosaleda In the gardens of the high part of the "Avinguda de la Diagonal".

Entry to Barcelona by the motorway where
it joins the ''Avinguda de la Diagonal''.

General view of part
of the University City

tant Barcelona citizens and subsidised by the Council, it contains
valuable works of art and is richly decorated. It can be visited
at certain times, and it is often used for exhibitions of works
of art belonging to the Patrimonio Nacional. Also adjacent to
the University City but on the right-hand side of the Avinguda de
la Diagonal is the Barcelona Football Club stadium. This
is undoubtedly one of the best sports constructions in the world
and a visit to it is a «must» for all who come to Barcelona. This
exceptional and admirable construction is the work of the
architects Francisco Mitjans Miró and José Soteras Mauri, aided
by the technicians D. Lorenzo, G. Barbón and F. Honestrosa.
Construction was started in 1954 and took three years to
complete. The great stadium with its annexes was inaugurated
on the 24 September 1957. The whole project was financed
by advance sales of season tickets and the emission of bonds and
debentures by the members of the Football Club themselves. The
stadium had capacity for 90.000 spectators.

The Plaza Françesc Macià and the Avinguda
de la Diagonal looking towards the centre of the c

With the motive of celebrating the World Cup Football 1982 in Spain, the football stadium ''Camp Nou'' was enlarged by putting a new floor on the stand, increasing its capacity to 120.000 spectators. The pitch is 110 by 75 metres, the maximum dimensions permitted by the regulations. The projecting roof of the tribune is 38 metres and is considered as singularly daring and technically well executed. The weight of the projection in iron is 550 tons.

The sports complex is formed by a ''Miniestadio'' with a capacity for 15.000 spectators, the functional style ''Palau Blaugrana I'' with a capacity for 5.000 spectators, central electronic scoreboard hung from a magnificent umbrella roof. It has access to the ramps of the stadium and also the entrance to the car park which has direct access to the grandstand. The influence and interest in basketball and hand-ball have found their maximum expression in these installations, not to mention hockey on skates and other indoor sports.

Pau Casals monument

The Plaza Françesc Maçià
another of Barcelona's
nerve-centres

The "Palau del Gel" (Ice Palace), another magnificent installation for exhibition skating and ice hockey is separated from the "Palau I" by a magnificent bar and the club offices, trophy room and other installations.

The "Palau Blaugrana II" in the same precint and next to "Travesera de las Corts" for indoor sports, has a capacity for 3.000 spectators and completes the sports complex.

Press Rooms, recreation rooms, dressing rooms, hockey pitches and five football pitches. Two well equiped gymnasiums with, parallel bars, rings, vaulting horses, etc., also used for Judo and Oriental sports. These are the installations which make up this magnificant complex which has more than 110.000 members.

Nearer the centre of the residential zone surrounding there is another important sporting installation. This is the football ground of the R.C.D. Español, with capacity for 40.000 spectators in Avinguda de la Diagonal de la Carretera de Sarriá. Although smaller both in dimensions and capacity than the club we have just described, it is still one of the most important sports centres of the city, both because of the history of the club and the category

The bull-ring «La Monumental»,
the biggest in Barcelona

The «paseillo» ot the toreros
and their quadrille, initial
ritual of all bullfights

Aerial view of the bull-ring «La
Monumental» just as a bullfight
is about to begin, with the
stands crowded with people

of the some of the matches played there during the season. The proof of this that although it has been enlarged as much as possible, it is still insufficient to accommodate all the spectators who try to get in. In this same area of the city there are other installations of a sporting character which are very important in the life of the city and which have also acquired international fame. Among such installations one must mention the Royal Polo Club at the end of the Avinguda de la Diagonal, the setting for very important horseriding shows and championships, and also equipped as a tennis club. Nearby in the street Capitán Martín Busutil in Pedralbes is the Royal Barcelona Tennis Club, world-famous for its international tennis tournaments, and the setting for year-round national championships. Also in the

The bull-ring «Las Arenas»

Avenida del Generalísimo are the fine new installations of the Royal Turó Tennis Club. Continuing down the Avenida towards the centre of the city, we come to the Plaza Françesc Macià, circular in form, with a large garden containing a pond in the centre of the square. As it is the focal point of several important roads, Plaça Françesc Macià is getting busier and more crowded with traffic every day, so that it is now one of the nerve-centres of the city life. It is made even busier by the many commercial and banking establishments surrounding it, as well as the high-quality restaurants, bars and places of entertainment one finds in the square itself and in adjacent streets. It is indeed the meeting-point of several streets where much of Barcelona's night life takes place — cabarets, «boites», dance-halls, restaurants serving excellent food, select bars — all of these may be found in streets leading into the Avenida del Generalísimo on one in streets leading into the Avinguda de la Diagonal on one side or other of the Plaza Françesc Macià. One of these streets. leading into the Avenida on the side nearer the centre of the city is calle Tuset, Barcelona's equivalent of Carnaby Street. We can safely say that the establishments in these streets lose nothing by comparison with similar places in London or any other foreign capital. Thus the tourist can be certain of finding places to provide him with a pleasant, amusing and unforgettable night in Barcelona. Continuing on down the Avinguda de la Diagonal, this time by day, we can turn right down any of the streets, all of which take us into the left-hand side of the Ensanche. It is worth paying at least a passing visit to this part, to help us get to know Barcelona better, discovering new aspects and details of the city. In this part of the Ensanche, in the street calle de Urgel, is the Universidad Industrial, one of the most effective teaching institutions of the city and deeply rooted in the industrial traditions of the country. In the same area we find the St George's Olympic Swimming Pool which was inaugurated only recently and which is admirable both for its facilities and its artistic decoration. In the calle de Casanova we find the Hospital Clínico, with its attached celebrated Medical Faculty. Since its foundation it has been one of the world's leading scientific centres where outstanding figures have lectured

The wonderful Barcelona Football Club Stadium, with a capacity for 120.000 spectators. In the centre the "Palau Blau Grana" and the "Palau de Gel" (Ice Palace). In the background the "Miniestadi" forming one of the best sports complexes in the world, built using the best and most modern techniques.

The Royal Barcelona
Tennis Club, scene of
national and
international
competitions
of world renown

and worked. The building was constructed by Doménech and
Estapé in 1904. On the dividing line between the old part of
the city and the Ensanche is the Plaza de la Universidad, with
the University Arts building. This latter is the work of the architect
Elías Rogent and was constructed between 1863 and 1873.
Rogent applied the Romanesque style of great and glorious
tradition in Cataluña, using it with sobriety, wisdom and elegance.
Not long ago it was declared of National interest and the gardens
surrounding it opened to the public. The building is rectangular
in form, 136 metres long and 83 wide. At each end there is an
identical high, square tower, recalling the best in medieval
architecture. Entering through the main doors we find ouselves
in a spacious, vaulted entrance-hall, with large niches in the
walls containing fine marble statues more than life-size. Those
of San Isidro, Averroes and Ramón Llull are by Venancio Vall-

mitjana, and those of Alfonso el Sabio and Lluis Vives by his brother Agapito Vallmitjana. From the left side of the hall the main staircase leads off up to the Rector's rooms and the auditorium. This latter contains murals by Baixeras, Ankermann, Bauzá and Reynés. On the opposité side from the auditorium is the University Library which contains some very important books and documents, including many published before the 16th century, plus 16th, 17th and 18th century documents from monastic libraries and archives destroyed in 1835. There are over 230,000 volumes in the library. Behind the University building is the Seminario Conciliar, constructed in the form of a cross and topped by a tower in imitation of that of the old Monastery of Poblet in the Province of Tarragona. The Seminario is also the work of Elías Rogent, but later than the main building. It also contains an important library. If we continue along Gran Via de les Corts Catalanes past the University, we quickly come to one of the most peaceful and finest promenades in Barcelona: the Rambla de Cataluña. Normally ideal for a relaxing stroll, this Rambla is also the setting for two of the liveliest, most picturesque

Municipal Palace of Sports at the entrance to Montjuic Park

Picornell Olympic
Swimming Pool in
Montjuïc Park, scene
of the European
Swimming Championships

and colourful festivals of the city. The first, just before Palm
Sunday in Holy Week, is when stalls selling elaborately prepared
palms and laurel are set up all along the Rambla. The other is
the traditional «fira de galls», or festival of chickens and turkeys
for the Christmas festivities, celebrated between the 21st and
25th December every year. We can now return to Gran Via de
les Corts Catalanes and continue on towards Paseo de Gracia, Between the Rambla and this Paseo there are some little gardens with
a monument to Eusebio Güell y Ferrer, the patron of many works
of art in the city. The monument is the work of Federico Marés.
There is also a slab with low reliefs and a medallion, with an
effigy of Francisco Soler y Rovirosa, the famous Catalan painter
and scenographer. So, surrounded by the modern and not-so-
modern buildings forming the crossroads of Gran Via de les Corts

Catalanes and Paseo de Gracia, the great fountain in the centre, with its powerful jets of water, we shall have returned to the Plaza de Cataluña.

We now wish to describe in more detail some of the many, varied tourist attractions in Barcelona which we have already mentioned briefly, as well as refer to others not yet described. So first of all we want to return to the subject of the bull-fights. In spite of all that one may believe to the contrary, Barcelona is the first city in Spain with respect to bull-fighting. And this refers not only to quantity but also quality. Every year in Barcelona, more than 200 bulls fight in the arenas, opposed by no

Montjuïc's Funfair, another popular venue
for nocturnal entertainment

less than 50 matadors, always including the most famous ones
of the moment. To celebrate what has been called the «Fiesta
Nacional», Barcelona has two big bull-rings : La Plaza de Toros
Las Arenas and La Plaza de Toros Monumental. The first was
inaugurated in June 1900, is the work of the architect Augusto
Font, and is in Plaza de España. It has capacity for 15,000
spectators, and has a privileged position in the history of bull-
fighting because of the long list of famous matadors, banderillos,
capeadors and picadors who have performed there. The Plaza
de Toros Monumental is at the other end of Gran Via de les Corts
Catalanes, on the corner of Paseo Carlos I, and has a capacity
of 19,600 spectators. Construction was begun in 1913 and
finished in 1916. Although of more recent construction than the
other one, it has become equally famous, and indeed is renowned
throughout the world for the important bull-fights which take
place there every year, attracting spectators of all nations avid
to witness the unique and picturesque spectacle offered by
bull-fighting. A unique and picturesque spectacle yes, but also
one which carries with it the constant possibility of death as
well as life. Life, gay and festive, in the parade of the quadrille,
in the fiery vitality of the bull and in the olés of applause for
the work of the capeador, for the torero's passes with the muleta

as he defies the beast; but death's constant menace in any and all of the manoevres with capa, chicuelina, verónica, farol and banderillas, in the passes with the muleta and the killing, which is when the torero comes to the moment of truth, administering the coup-de-grace to the bull. To wander at night along the Ramblas, the Avinguda del Paral·lel, and the districts around the port is to enjoy the spectacle of Barcelona by night. The Ramblas at night retain their poetic and very personal quality. Artificial light gives the trees, the flower-stalls and the newspaper kiosks a different magic from that which they have in the daytime, and the crowds are still there. If the tourist wants organised entertainment for his evening out, Barcelona has plenty to offer him: he can see festivals of folklore, Andalusian or Flamenco shows, variety theatres, music-halls, cabarets, night-clubs and dance-halls. All of this can be found in the Ramblas themselves or in adjacent streets, or in the high part of town in the sector between the Plaza Francesc Macià and the celebrated Tuset Street. There are other simi-

View of part of the
course at the Royal
Golf Club of the Prat

Aerial view of the San
Sebastián beach, one
of the most popular
in the city

lar places along the Avinguda de la Diagonal on the other side of
Françesc Macià. Then there is also the possibility of an amusing,
light-hearted evening in Montjuïc's Funfair which continues
functioning until the early hours of the morning. And in addition
to Flamenco singing and dancing and the widest variety of other
kinds of show, our tourist can enjoy from the best and most
authentic red wines to the most famous exotic liqueurs in the
world. Barcelona also offers a varied selection of places for
tasty meals, ranging from typical taverns around the harbour
up to high-class restaurants of national and international fame,
distributed in and around Barcelona. Barcelona has an excellent
gastronomic tradition and can pride itself on being able to offer

the gourmet an outstanding and varied selection of succulent dishes including examples of Catalan, Provençal, Valencian and Aragonese cuisines. This variety is very useful as each cuisine offers dishes which can be enjoyed at different seasons of the year. In spring for example there are «habas a la catalana» (broad beans), «salmonetes a la brasa», «lubinas» (bass) and «Mero» (grouper) in «suquet», a sort of fish fricassee, and rice with fish; in summer, the typical salads, vegetables, cold or grilled lobster, rabbit with «all i oli» (a very tasty garlic sauce) and «sanfaina» which consists of a sort of stew of tomatoes, cucumber, celery, radish, carrots and other vegetables with meat,

To have a good time in your leisure hours, Barcelona also has its dance-halls, boites...

... and cabarets, music-halls, and other places offering the most varied of entertainments, dancing, acrobatics, review and amusing comedies, to cater for the tastes of all who wish to enjoy their evenings in Barcelona

Neither is it difficult to see
and hear Flamenco in
Barcelona at night: these
songs and dances are
featured in special places
where the most famous
exponents of genuine
Andalusian folklore perform

Aerial view — St. Pablo Hospital —.

or cod, or pigs' trotters, and accompanied by chicken; in autumn, partridge with Brussels sprouts, hare with chestnuts, and quail in all its varieties; and in winter, pigs' trotters and the» escudella i carn d'olla», as well as roast chicken with dates, pine-seeds and raisins. And one mustn't forget that Spanish charcuterie, offering a selection which can be combined with many other dishes, is of high quality; or that all varieties of fruit are available throughout the year.

Barcelona's very modern airport, setting for welcomes and fond farewells, can serve as the point of departure for this guide. A lot of work has recently been done on it so that it is now equipped with the most modern of runways for the most powerful of aeroplanes with the corresponding services and installations.

The reception hall is both functional and magnificent, with its grandiose proportions and striking artistic decoration. This decoration includes murals, mosaics, stained glass and reliefs, by artists such as Vaquero Turcios and Maciá and those of the Escuela Massana. The main façade features an enormous mural by the artist Joan Miró and the ceramicist Llorenç Artigas, and set in the gardens beside the approach road to the main building there is a great wrought iron statue of Don Quijote riding Clavileño el Aligero, the wooden flying horse. The artist was Ros Sabater.

Barcelona seen by night
from the Tibidabo mountain